RESEARCHING ONLINE

adapted by

Christopher Busiel and Tom Maeglin

from

Teaching Online: Internet Research,
Conversation, and Composition

by

Daniel Anderson, Bret Benjamin,
Christopher Busiel, and Bill Paredes-Holt

Longman Resources for Instructors

An imprint of Addison Wesley Longman, Inc.

New York • Reading, Massachusetts • Menlo Park, California • Harlow, England
Don Mills, Ontario • Sydney • Mexico City • Madrid • Amsterdam

Researching Online, adapted by Christopher Busiel and Tom Maeglin

ISBN: 0-321-01960-1

1 2 3 4 5 6 7 8 9 10 - ML - 00 99 98 97

Preface

Researching Online has been adapted from *Teaching Online: Internet Research, Conversation, and Composition* by Daniel Anderson, Bret Benjamin, Christopher Busiel, and Bill Paredes-Holt. *Teaching Online* has helped many instructors prepare writing courses that utilize the Internet. Many have suggested that a briefer version could serve students after they left the classroom to pursue their research projects. This handy reference seeks to guide students in using the principal Internet media when defining and narrowing topics, gathering information, collaborating with others who have similar interests, and writing the results and conclusions.

Each chapter briefly describes at least one Internet medium, orienting the reader to the key terms and issues that relate to it, and explaining how the medium is used for research. Chapter 1 describes some of the benefits and dangers of conducting research on the Internet and briefly describes some of the technologies that form the backdrop for the tools that are the focus of subsequent chapters. Chapter 2, "Initiating Conversation: E-Mail," discusses electronic mail and Listservs. E-mail is a building block of Internet communication, a tool that can transform both student interaction and research. Chapter 3, "Usenet News," looks at Usenet newsgroups, focusing on their benefits for defining and narrowing topics and emphasizing the importance of critical reading skills. Chapter 4, "Real-time Discussion: IRCs and MU*s," discusses Internet Relay Chat and Multi User Domains—text-based spaces which allow "real-time" conversation and the construction of virtual environments. The chapter includes two lists providing basic IRC and MU* commands. Chapter 5, "The Electronic Library: Browsing with Gopher and the World Wide Web," looks at "browsing" the Internet for resources. It considers a variety of strategies for successfully finding and evaluating Internet research materials and describes a variety of web research tools. Chapter 6, "Node Construction Ahead: The Web and Hypertext Markup Language," explains the basics of HyperText Markup Language (HTML) for posting research projects. Chapter 7 gives guidelines for documenting Internet or "electronic" sources in both MLA and ACW style. An appendix considers copyright issues on the Internet. A Glossary of Internet terms and an index end the guide.

All chapters have been updated to reflect the growth and changes that have characterized the Internet since the publication of *Teaching Online*. URLs and other addresses are current as the guide goes to press.

Acknowledgments

Thanks go first to the coauthors of *Teaching Online*, Daniel Anderson, Bret Benjamin, and Bill Paredes-Holt, without whose efforts on that text, and their invaluable advice since its publication, *Researching Online* would not be possible. Thanks also to Jane Aaron who provided valuable suggestions for refining the adaptation.

At Longman, Patricia Rossi guided the project and Donna Campion brought all its elements together. John Callahan designed a brilliant cover. Tita Chico wondrously turned the manuscript into something lovely. We thank them all.

Finally, we thank our friends and family for their love and support. Tom thanks Phoebe Cooper and Sam and Daphne Maeglin for the joy they bring every day. Chris thanks Joanne, George, and Erika Busiel for their strength in trying times.

CONTENTS

CHAPTER 1

Introduction

The Information Superhighway. The Network of Networks. Virtual Reality. Cyberspace. The Hive. The New Frontier. The Global Village. The Electronic Town Hall.

The Internet.

The past few years have seen unparalleled media coverage of the Internet, touting it as an unlimited resource and an egalitarian, world-wide forum. Of course if you've been online, you are probably aware that the realities do not necessarily match the hype. Resources can be difficult to locate, and the overwhelming amount of vapid—even offensive—information on the Internet can make online experiences disorienting and disturbing. As for being universal and egalitarian, recent statistics suggest that the vast majority of Internet users are white American males affiliated with institutions of higher education.

RESEARCH, CONVERSATION AND COMPOSITION

While an Internet utopia remains unlikely, this enormous network does, after all, contain countless texts offering researchers new opportunities for scholarship. For students who are working in a computer classroom or at home, the net offers access to documents located around the world. Additionally, the Internet itself can be thought of as an enormous, constantly evolving conversation in which users meet to discuss almost any imaginable topic. There are dozens of ways you can benefit from using the Internet; for instance, you could easily:

- Access important information to support your research.
- Communicate with authors of important sources or experts in various fields of study.
- Meet online with other researchers to discuss a common topic.
- Design and "publish" an interactive, multimedia site on the World Wide Web, offering a research paper, links to further Internet resources about the topic, video clips of major figures, and forums for conversation among users.

Because of the vast amounts and the wide variety of information that it provides, the Internet can be an excellent medium for honing your research skills. Whether you perform keyword searches on a global scale or access a single database, the wealth of materials available makes focusing topics, evaluating and documenting sources, and developing strategies for locating information all necessary requirements of working effectively with the net. Additionally, materials found online will often differ a great deal from those in print. Resources may feature graphics, sound, and video, for example. What's more, Internet sources may have a more (or less) impressive appearance than traditional "published" articles. These new media present researchers with the challenge of deciding what constitutes source material.

This challenge necessitates critical reading. For example, any particular Listserv (see Chapter Two) might contain news messages from wire services, in-depth reports from independent journalists or academics who have done a great deal of research on a topic, and any combination of less authoritative messages. Because traditional requirements of expertise do not exist for electronic "publishing," many previously marginalized voices find audiences on the Internet. While increasing the number of perspectives can to some degree democratize access to information, this diversity requires greater attention to source evaluation and provides a more complex understanding of an issue.

This guide will provide detailed information about possible Internet tools for research, and enough practical advice to implement those tools successfully in your work.

SOME THINGS TO KEEP IN MIND

You should be aware of some of the problems presented by the Internet, so that you can overcome them in your research. Among the problems you should be aware of when using the Internet are the following:

- the temptation to play online and the risk of losing sight of your purpose
- the vast volume of information on the Internet and the difficulties of managing it
- the steep learning curve and prohibitive expense of some applications and Internet technologies.
- the fact that, despite its global scale, the Internet (and indeed to personal computers in general) is still heavily marked by class, race, gender, and geography.

Always try to determine whether the extra work or expense of certain Internet media merits their use on a particular project. If you master a few basic operations of Internet applications, learn a few strategies for finding and evaluating sources, and keep focused while online, chances are the Internet will reward you for your efforts.

CLIENT/SERVER INTERACTION

Central to the Internet are the concepts of the *client* and the *server*. Although it is common to think of an Internet server as an actual computer, in reality servers are programs which reside on network-connected machines. What distinguishes a server program from other software is that it provides files and information for use by client programs. These clients are a separate set of programs which "talk" to servers and access the data they offer according to specific *protocols* which act as a sort of "language" between Internet clients and servers. Internet media are distinguished by the types of protocols they follow. For example, a mail reading client accesses a mail server using the shared language of SMTP (Simple Mail Transfer Protocol), or similarly, an FTP client and server interact using File Transfer Protocol. All of the Internet applications we discuss require that your local machine have some sort of connection with an Internet server.

Though some of the Internet functions will vary, a user has three basic options for accessing information on the net. For example, when reading e-mail a user could
- telnet to a shell on a mainframe and log on to the machine's mail server.
- telnet to a shell on a mainframe and activate a mailreading client that resides on that machine.
- operate a mailreading client located on her own personal computer. Throughout the book we refer to these programs as "workstation clients."

Although very basic, Telnet is among the most versatile of Internet clients in that it can communicate with servers using a number of different protocols. Thus, Telnet facilitates a wide range of activities with a very simple computer system. You can connect to Telnet servers (like library catalogs and other databases), MUD servers or mail servers. (Note that in common usage, the term "Telnet" both describes the process of making Internet connections and denotes the name of client applications which perform this function, such as NCSA Telnet and Trumpet Telnet.) A simple Telnet connection to a remote server does not, however, provide an intuitive interface and often requires that you know a number of specialized commands. Additionally, Telnet connections offer very few features for archiving your interactions.

Client programs that can be operated through the use of a Telnet connection provide a user with greater flexibility than the Telnet connection alone. Through Telnet, you can log on to an account on an Internet-connected computer and activate various client programs which reside there. For example, you could connect to remote mail and news reading clients and use their easier interface to read, compose, and store messages. In addition, users often access remote clients to navigate MUDs much more efficiently. Many accounts also provide a Gopher client, and some provide limited access to the World Wide Web using Lynx, a text-only Web browser. While all of these remote client programs offer greater utility than a direct Telnet connection to a server, they are still less "friendly" than workstation client software.

If at all possible, you should use workstation client software. These are programs that operate on your personal computer and control your interface with Internet servers. The drawback to this type of client software is that these programs often require a faster Internet connection (especially for newsreaders and graphical Web browsers) and a more powerful personal computer. But in return, workstation client software offers an easy interface that lets you concentrate less on the technology and more on what you want to do with the technology. Besides making Internet operations almost transparent, workstation client software offers the best features for viewing, retrieving, saving, storing, and composing.

The client programs themselves are simple to install and readily available as *freeware* and *shareware*. (Freeware programs are available for public use without charge; shareware is available with the request of payment in good faith of a small licensing fee for use of their software.) You can obtain copies of Internet client software at a number of FTP sites listed in the next section.

The following chapters suggest a few workstation client software programs (for either Macintosh or Windows-based systems) for each Internet medium. Remember, these applications and their operations can be revised and improved by the programmers at any time, so look periodically for the latest version of the client software you need.

BASIC FUNCTIONS: TELNET AND FILE TRANSFER PROTOCOL (FTP)

Telnet is a terminal emulation protocol: with a Telnet client you can establish a connection to a remote computer, almost like being at the machine's keyboard. Once connected, a user can work with files in a specific portion of the computer's operating system (a "shell"), access files being shared by a server program, or activate other client programs that reside on the remote machine. You can download Telnet client applications, like NCSA Telnet and Trumpet Telnet, as freeware from a variety of sites, or sometimes obtain them directly from your institution.

A Telnet connection is the most basic of all Internet functions. Before media like Gopher and the Web were available, researchers often used Telnet applications to connect directly to a site which offered a specific kind of database. An example of such a site is *info.umd.edu* at the University of Maryland. It offers an electronic archive of government documents (from the text of legislative bills to transcripts of presidential press conferences), and thus is still an excellent resource. While you might still use a Telnet application to connect directly to such sites, more and more archives are making their text files available through Gopher or the Web.

A user has two basic options for using a Telnet client to access information on the net. For example, when reading e-mail a user could:

- Telnet to a shell on a mainframe and log on to the machine's mail server in order to read text files directly from the server.
- Telnet to a shell on a mainframe and activate a mailreading client that resides on that machine. This remote client program will offer the reader an improved interface for managing mail. Note, however, that this interface is still limited by the simplicity of the Telnet connection.

If you use other workstation client software, you will probably not make extensive use of Telnet applications, or make direct Telnet connections yourself.

File Transfer Protocol (FTP) is a basic means by which files - -including text files, graphics, even applications themselves—are downloaded from and uploaded to central sites by users working at their desktop computers. Because FTP client programs can be used to download Internet software, they should be one of the first applications you obtain (probably from your computation center). Transferring files can be a difficult process (though made easier by client programs), and we do not have the opportunity here to explain it fully. Some of the issues you will need to be concerned with are: knowing the address of a site which contains the materials you want, negotiating the directory structure on that site, choosing the right settings for downloading the files, and decompressing these files to produce the resources you desire. Your institution may maintain its own FTP site with appropriate programs for your system.

You can find Internet client software at many FTP sites including the following:

- *ftp.utexas.edu* (Mac only)
- *dartvax.dartmouth.edu*
- *wuarchive.wustl.edu*
- *ftp.ncsa.uiuc.edu*
- *sumex-aim.stanford.edu*

Although file transfers can be performed with programs resident on institutional servers (often by typing *ftp* and an address at the prompt), we strongly recommend that you look into client software for this procedure— it will alleviate many of the difficulties involved in transferring files. Most of these applications also allow you to save site addresses, login names, and directory paths as bookmarks, so you can return to especially useful sites with one click of the mouse. Two common FTP client programs are Fetch (for Macintosh systems) and WS_FTP (for Windows systems).

Because files on FTP sites are sometimes *compressed* (rewritten in a way that consumes less memory) in a variety of different formats, you will probably need to have on hand several different applications for decompression. The format used for decompression will be indicated by the filename's suffix (the last part of the file name following a period, for example, *.sit*, *.tar*, *.zip*). If you do not have decompression software, you will want to look for *self-extracting archives* (ending with the suffix *.sea*), which require no decompression software; unfortunately, however, a lot of material is not compressed using this method. Decompression software is available around the Internet for downloading, but tends to be shareware rather than freeware. You will have to compromise between your needs for downloading and the licensing fees you can afford. Speak with your systems administrator about the decompression software you might need for particular files, as well as how to obtain and configure client software for FTP.

You may also use FTP for uploading files to a server, as, for example, in publishing World Wide Web documents. When loading files, make sure that HTML documents and any text files are sent as "ASCII text" or "text only" and that other media are transported as "binary" or "raw data." Also make sure that file names remain unaltered during the uploading process. You may need to turn off settings on the FTP client application which append extensions to the file names.

6

CHAPTER 2

Initiating Conversation: E-Mail

WHAT IS E-MAIL?

If the Internet can be described as a continuously evolving conversation, then electronic mail isthe basic technology that allows you to speak up and be heard. E-mail is a building block of Internet communication and composition. The audience for e-mail messages can encompass a single instructor or student, a group of students, the class as a whole, a campus e-mail discussion list, or a world-wide audience made up of personal contacts or subscribers to a Listserv.

The basic tool for sending and receiving e-mail is called a mailreader (also known as a "mail client"). While it may be possible to exchange e-mail without a mailreader, these programs provide an easy interface for reading, composing, posting and downloading e-mail messages. Common mailreaders include Eudora (for Macintosh systems) and Weudora (for Windows and DOS systems respectively). While it is common for Internet service providers (ISP's) to provide a mailreader in their basic package, it is easy to find many other mailreaders with different features and characteristics. Many mailreader programs can be downloaded from the Internet as freeware (software programs distributed free of charge). Of course, many other mailreader programs are available wherever software is sold.

Mailreaders do not exchange messages with one another directly. Rather, they send and receive messages through mail servers, computers connected to the Internet which organize, store and distribute e-mail messages to various users. Servers exchange with each other (often with many other servers relaying the messages in-between) using two-part e-mail addresses.

ADDRESSES AND THEIR ELEMENTS

A typical e-mail address contains two elements. The *mailbox name* or *user's name* appears before the @ sign, and the domain information, representing the server that provides e-mail to the user, follows the @ sign. A sample message might use the addresses:

    From: bozo@archives.widgetinc.com
    To: bilbo@mail.utexas.edu

The *mailbox name* of the sender is bozo. The recipient's mailbox name is bilbo.

The *domain* generally contains information about the organization and organization type. Elements of the domain are separated by a period (.) generally called a "dot".

The first sample's, domain includes the machine name, "archives," the name of the organization, "widgetinc" and an abbreviation describing the type of organization, "com" (commercial). The mailbox of the recipient, bilbo, is operated by the machine name "mail," registered with the organization "utexas," classified as "edu" (educational).

In the United States, the standard domain types are
.edu = educational institution
.com = commercial organization
.gov = government organization
.mil = military institution
Outside the United States, domain names usually end in a two-letter element indicating the country of origin: for example, .jp (Japan), .nl (the Netherlands), and .eg (Egypt).

Many mailreaders allow you to save addresses in a file called an address book which makes it unnecessary to retype an address. In addition, many provide ways to keep special addresses called nicknames on file. A *nickname* is a list of addresses represented by one name. When a message is sent to the nickname, the computer sends that message to each of the addresses in the nickname file.

WHAT IS A LISTSERV?

A Listserv, also known as a "mailing list" or "list," is a program which allows e-mail to be sent to a group of addresses simultaneously. (Throughout this text we will use the term "Listserv" generically to denote a range of mailing list programs including Listserv, Majordomo and Listproc.) Though Listservs vary according to function, type, and administration, each Listserv has a very narrowly defined subject area to which subscribers are expected to adhere in their posts. For example, the discussion list MODBRITS carefully defines its scope as "Modern British and Irish Literature: 1895-1955," and participants are expected to abide by the list's geographic and chronological limits, or provide a good rationale for ranging outside them.

Listserv users should consider conventions of Internet etiquette, or "netiquette." One does not usually send a message to a list just to pass the time or to try to sell a car (unless the list is for the purpose of selling used cars). For most lists, posts like this would be frowned upon and would result in a number of angry messages (or *flames*) from list members. Some lists have moderators who screen messages before sending them to the full list in order to ensure their relevance. Repeated inflammatory or "off-topic" messages from a user can result in removal from the list. Listservs pose the problems of interaction with a large audience and previous discussions on the list.

Following a Listserv discussion can clarify the nature of the Listserv's audience and reveal eventually what constitutes an interesting or convincing message on that list. Sometimes, the boundaries of allowable topics on a list are very narrowly defined. For example, the **h-latam** list (a discussion of Latin American history) specifically defines its subject to exclude current events in Latin America. Because the list perceives its function as providing a level-headed discussion of "historical" events, especially as these relate to teaching history, potentially heated political discussions of more recent events in Latin America are therefore discouraged. A post discussing causes and effects of the Zapatista uprising in Chiapas, Mexico, for instance, would not be allowed on the list unless it was directed solely to bibliographic source material or pedagogical concerns.

FORMS AND FORMALITY: HOW IS E-MAIL DIFFERENT FROM TRADITIONAL WRITING?

By its nature, e-mail tends to be less formal than traditional composition. Messages often contain unedited typographical errors and abbreviations like *BTW* ("by the way"), *FWIW* ("for what it's worth") or *IMHO* ("in my humble opinion"), *msg* ("message"), *mtg* ("meeting") or *shd* ("should"). The ability to send and receive messages quickly using e-mail has de-emphasized the importance of carefully constructed prose generally found in other forms of correspondence. In fact, e-mail can be compared more closely with spoken conversation than with its more obvious counterpart, letter writing.

However, since e-mail lacks certain qualities of face-to-face interaction — gestures, mannerisms, intonations — Internet conversationalists have developed additional conventions of expression: emoticons, signature files, and reply quotations.

Expressing sarcasm and lighthearted emotion is often achieved by using *emoticons* (usually called "*smileys*"). Though they often denote the lack of careful writing that irony requires, smileys do communicate something

9

about the author's intention. The basic smiley is a sideways happy face : -) although a whole host of others can be used to express a broad range of emotions. Understand that manipulating these forms is part of e-mail communication. Though a writer might incorporate a smiley in informal prose, it would be preferable in a formal composition to use words to convey irony effectively.

A SMALL SAMPLING OF SMILEYS

:-)	basic smiley	C=:-)	chef smiley
;-)	winking happy smiley	8(:-)	Mickey Mouse
;-(	crying smiley	:——}	you lie like pinnochio
:-{	mustache	[:-)	smiley wearing a walkman
:-}X smiley	bow tie-wearing	X:-)	little kid with a propeller beanie
@:-}	smiley just back from the hairdresser		

Taken from **ftp://ftp.wwa.com/pub/Scarecrow/Misc/Smilies**

Another way of personalizing e-mail communication is by adding a *signature* or *sig file* to a message. A signature is a section of text automatically appended to the bottom of e-mail messages. Signatures serve as a way to identify the author and place her socially, professionally, and personally. Besides supplying the writer's e-mail address to facilitate replies, a signature will often carry a writer's professional or academic affiliations, an indication of whether the current message is personal or professional, or a favorite quotation. To lighten this rather dry information, many authors have developed elaborate arrangements of text and symbols in their signatures.

ASCII ART IN A SIGNATURE FILE

```
("`_''-/").___..__''"._JohnDoe@mail.utexas.edu
 `6_ 6  )   `-.  (     ).`-.__.`)       John Doe
 (_Y_.)'  ._   )  `._ `. ``-..-'  Department of
  _..`--'_..-_/  /--'_.' ,'        Nomenclature
(il),-'' (li),'  ((!.-'
```

Although widespread, signature files have not been wholly accepted by all Internet users. As a result, plays upon the signature file abound. One of the most succinct signature files, dutifully attached at the end of many messages, is "This is not a signature."

Another e-mail convention arose because of the ease with which computer technology reproduces text. When you reply to an e-mail message, you can usually include the original message in the response. The e-mail convention for quoting text uses an angle bracket (>) to indicate the text that is quoted from the original message. Most mailreaders automatically quote the whole text of the preceding message into their reply, so reply quotations can be quite long and include lots of extraneous information.

REPLY QUOTATION

```
          To: student@mail.utexas.edu
        From: instructor@mail.utexas.edu
     Subject: Re:  Can we meet?
          Cc:
         Bcc:
 Attachments:
.......................................................................
 >Howdy Instructor,
 >
 >I was writing to see if we could set up
 >a meeting to talk about the paper that's
 >due on Friday. I have to work on Tuesday
 >during your office hours, so I was wondering
 >if we could set up a time on Wednesday?  You
 >can mail me back or call at 555-5000. Thanks.
 >
 >John Doe

 No problem John.  I can meet with you in the
 morning between 9 and 10:30 or in the
 afternoon after 2:00.  Drop me a line and tell
 me if either of those times is OK with you.

 Instructor
```

Each time a messages is quoted, an additional angle bracket will appear before each line of the text. This nesting of quotations continues until one reader decides that there is no need to include the older text, and deletes it. Because e-mail messages are read with varying frequency by different users, some think it necessary to include the original question or issue for clarity. While an unnecessarily long reply quotation can be an annoyance, it can be useful to "overhear" part of the original conversation, or to analyze the original message a second time. Consider cutting out the less significant portions of the reply quotation, to draw your correspondent's attention to the material you consider most important; contextualize this material in your response.

LEARNING TO TALK, TALKING TO LEARN

Your instructors may create class Listservs or nicknames to make announcements, revise reading or meeting schedules, forward supplementary material, start discussion, or ask for feedback on a particular topic. Lists and nicknames also give students the opportunity to contribute material for course reading and to share relevant resources with the entire class.

Joining conversations outside of the classroom will illustrate the commitments of writers to their discussion of issues and ideas, and will demonstrate that your writing can be important in a larger context. Using Listservs can give you access to the opinions of experts. This access to information is a useful stimulus for creating a topic and finding a way to enter a conversation. For example, depending on the Listserv, you might come across an index of sources about a research topic or gather extremely current information on a contemporary debate or event.

As we demonstrate below on page 16, a variety of resources can be accessed through electronic mail, many of which differ from traditional research materials. The multiplicity of voices in Listserv debates provides uncommon resources.

Besides drawing on the conversations of subscribers to a list, e-mail offers the ability to interact with members of the list. You can ask questions, post your own opinions and receive reactions to the arguments you are developing for class. This interaction will provide you with reactions to your arguments from perspectives outside the classroom. This process highlights the need for you to write clearly, responsibly and knowledgeably. If a message asks an obvious question or appears to ask the list to do your research for you, the message will likely receive some hostile responses and few, if any, useful replies. But if you are able to engage the audience with either an interesting argument or an important category of research or analysis, you will likely receive many useful citations and suggestions for further thought. Because of the nature of electronic communication, all of these messages can easily be archived on a diskette and retrieved for later use. Messages can also be forwarded to an instructor, other students, or people outside the classroom.

GETTING CONNECTED

We recommend that all students set up an e-mail account. Most colleges and universities have already incorporated computer and Internet fees into tuition costs, so they generally offer "free" or very inexpensive e-mail accounts to students and faculty. Although some students will inevitably have problems along the way, setting up an account is usually a fairly simple process.

Setting up an e-mail account may take a little time, so request your account very early in the semester. Learn about your systems by reading any handouts with detailed step-by-step instructions. Since schools frequently change e-mail procedures from semester to semester as they expand their computer services, bear in mind that some of the instructions may be incorrect. To verify that your account is working, send yourself a test message.

WHAT ARE MAILREADERS AND SERVERS?

Mail servers are programs which reside on Internet-connected machines which store and distribute electronic messages. A user has three basic options for accessing these servers:

1. The most basic, but also the most limited, way to work with e-mail is through a connection to a remote machine's mail server via a Telnet client. It is possible to read and send messages with this connection; however, the interface is quite awkward.

2. Most users will prefer to use a mail-reading client when working with e-mail. Making a Telnet connection to a remote machine and activating a mail-reading client provides an easier interface and offers more features to the user than connecting directly to the mail server. For example the main menu of Pine, a Unix-based mailreader, looks like this:

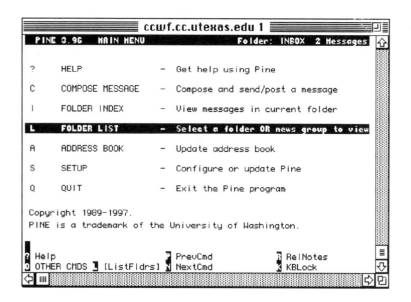

In this format, a variety of functions can be performed with keystrokes. The reader's mail remains on the server, but saved messages can be sorted into folders. An address book feature allows quick access to frequently-used addresses.

3. Workstation mail-reading clients reside on the user's personal computer and provide the most versatile interface for handling e-mail operations. These programs (Eudora is probably the most popular and is available as freeware) retrieve mail from the mail server and bring it to a user's machine. Like server-based mailreaders, workstation clients allow users to create nicknames, and offer features like the ability to send formatted documents as attachments and to organize incoming mail into directories or mailboxes for later use. The main difference between these types of mailreaders is that with a workstation client, the user has access to a variety of mouse-driven menu commands and other features. Mail reading and composition are done in multiple, separate windows. New messages are easily composed, edited, sent and saved. Looking at a portion of a sample composition window (our reply quotation example from above), note a number of features:

14

```
┌─────────────────────────────────────────────────┐
│ ▤⬜▤  student@mail.utexas.edu, Re: Can u ▤⬜▤     │
├─────────────────────────────────────────────────┤
│  ⬜  │BIN│  ✓ QP  ▣ ⬚ →| ⬚ ⚡  ( Queue )         │
│      │HEX│                                        │
├─────────────────────────────────────────────────┤
│      To: student@mail.utexas.edu            ⬆    │
│    From: instructor@mail.utexas.edu         ▤    │
│ Subject: Re:  Can we meet?                  ▤    │
│      Cc:                                    ▦    │
│     Bcc:                                    ▦    │
│ Attachments:                                ▦    │
│ ⋯⋯⋯⋯⋯⋯⋯⋯⋯⋯⋯⋯⋯⋯⋯⋯⋯⋯⋯⋯⋯⋯⋯⋯⋯⋯⋯⋯⋯⋯⋯⋯⋯⋯⋯⋯⋯⋯⋯⋯   │
│ >Howdy Instructor,                          ▦    │
└─────────────────────────────────────────────────┘
```

By clicking on items across the top bar, the user can set such features as "text-wrap" at the end of lines, as well as automatically save a copy of the message in her "outgoing" mailbox, and control whether or not to use her signature file (which Eudora saves for her in another window). The button which reads "queue" prepares this message for mailing, but the outgoing message will not be sent until the user selects a menu command to send all her queued messages. This feature is useful if you want to minimize the time you are actually connected to the Internet (if a modem and a phone share the same line, for example, or your Internet access is billed by the minute). If the user were to change a particular setting, the "queue" button would instead say "send," and clicking it would deliver the message immediately.

Information about your account is easily saved by workstation mailreaders like Eudora:

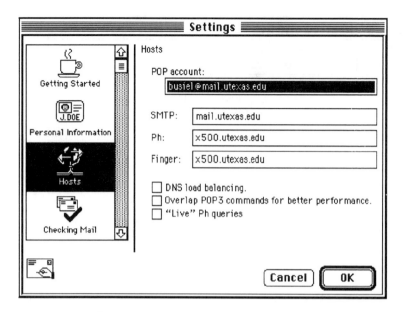

Settings

Getting Started

Personal Information

Hosts

Checking Mail

Hosts

POP account:
busiel@mail.utexas.edu

SMTP: mail.utexas.edu

Ph: x500.utexas.edu

Finger: x500.utexas.edu

☐ DNS load balancing.
☐ Overlap POP3 commands for better performance.
☐ "Live" Ph queries

[Cancel] [OK]

Once you set up the information you will never have to retype your e-mail address, your signature file or other information. You will always have access to the configurations, however, so you can continue modifying the mailreader's functions to your liking.

Classroom Uses for e-mail

You can use e-mail in any of the following ways:
- connecting with members of the class on an individual basis, and with the instructor outside of class and office hours. E-mail can be especially useful when an unexpected problem or question arises, or when other settings are inappropriate or uncomfortable for asking the question.
- making inquiries to the instructor, if you have missed class or have a question about an assignment.
- turning in papers or other homework, to which instructors can respond by e-mailing comments back to you.
- receiving materials particularly relevant to a project, from Listservs, browsing sessions (see chapter five), other students or your instructor.

E-mail is also an invaluable tool for any number of group activities:
- Peer review partners can e-mail each other their drafts and comments with the advantage of being able to ask questions and carry on a dialogue.

16

- Small groups working on collective projects can use e-mail to brainstorm about ideas, to share work that they have completed individually, or to coordinate times to meet as a group.
- Students who have similar research topics can use e-mail to exchange resources and materials that they have found.

HOW CAN I USE E-MAIL FOR GATHERING RESOURCES?

E-mail can serve as an important research tool. By using e-mail to connect with a larger audience, you can learn from the expertise and creative thinking of others.

The first, and probably the most important, way that e-mail can be applied to research is by subscribing to Listservs. Listservs with wide subscription circles can be an important source of both resource materials and a range of positions on a given issue. You can subscribe to any of literally thousands of topic-based Listservs according to your personal interests, or coinciding with course topics. These lists range in traffic anywhere from a trickle to fifty or more messages per day. The types of information posted on lists also vary widely; some lists limit themselves to news stories and articles, while others are dedicated solely to discussion.

As a result, it is difficult to judge the traits of a list without subscribing. Instructors in the field you are writing about will often have helpful suggestions about good Listservs in that area. Also, the Web site *http://tile.net/Listserv/* contains some useful descriptions and information about a number of Listservs (see Chapter 5 for information about finding resources on the World Wide Web).

Although these descriptions are a helpful start, in the end you will need to trust your judgment to decide for yourself the quality and usefulness of any particular list.

You should exercise caution in joining a Listserv. You should spend time reading the list, or "lurking," before attempting to join the conversation. In addition, it pays to review the list's *frequently asked questions (FAQs)* file, which can answer basic questions and illuminate the nature of the list. To avoid an overly hostile response to any careless postings, prepare your messages carefully. Also familiarize yourself with the basics of netiquette before subscribing to a list.

For gathering substantive research material, the most useful lists are those posting items like news stories, articles, documents, and expert commentary. However, you should not give up on a list simply because it focuses on discussion, for you can learn a lot by keeping track of and participating in active Listserv debates. You will see how opinions are formed, revised, and complicated, and how multiple perspectives can inform a topic.

Discussion lists provide an excellent opportunity to practice critical reading. Because of the nontraditional nature of some e-mail sources, readers are forced to examine and analyze both the content and the style of Listserv postings. Examining messages from a variety of Listserv discussions can put in plain view the importance of writing for a particular audience. You will see in these public debates practical applications of the rhetorical skills you learn in class. Notice also how Listserv members observe (or fail to observe) the rules of netiquette and the effects this has on the ongoing discussion.

Along with the research possibilities provided by Listservs, e-mail can be an effective tool for transferring and gathering other types of information. For instance, many online library catalogs and databases allow users to mail information to their accounts. When you find a useful online articles, for instance, you can collect that information easily by e-mailing yourself the material. Once you receive the material in electronic form, you can refer back to the piece at a later date or cut and paste quotations into your paper (with proper acknowledgment, of course).

CHAPTER 3

Usenet News

WHAT ARE USENET NEWSGROUPS?

Similar to private bulletin boards and commercial message sites, newsgroups are topic-specific sites of discussion and news distribution. Your school will most likely be connected to Usenet, an enormous network of groups from around the world. The broad classification of Usenet contains thousands of topic-centered newsgroups organized hierarchically by name. The server at your school (the *news server*, or *news host*) collects and organizes the groups. You will access newsgroups with a *news reader* (or *news client*), which provides an easy interface for reading, composing, posting, and downloading newsgroup messages.

Messages (or *posts*) displayed by the news reader are varied. Many come from other Usenet users like yourself. Others may be *news feeds*, or messages posted to a newsgroup by a wire service or other traditional news source. (As you see from the preceding sentences, the word *post* can be used as either a noun or a verb.) The newsgroup messages form threads, consisting of an original posting and a series of replies on the same topic, usually with the same subject heading. The "news" at a typical Usenet newsgroup is a mixture of multimedia, personal postings, carefully crafted articles, and conventional news feeds. The groups not only distribute these topic-centered materials, but also fulfill an important social function by providing spaces where individuals can meet and engage in discussion.

Most World Wide Web browsers now incorporate newsreading interfaces that coordinate the reading and composition of newsgroup posts (see Chapter Five). If you do not have access to the Web and a browser, you have other options for accessing newsgroups. The most basic news reading option is a client program residing on a remote Internet-connected machine. By Telnetting to an Internet account and activating a news reading client, a user can read and respond to newsgroup messages. A more user-friendly form of newsreader operates from the machines of individual workstations. These workstation clients allow users to customize lists of groups and offer searching, decoding and other capabilities. Some common news readers are Newswatcher and Nuntius (for Macintosh) and WinVN and Trumpet News (for Windows).

19

At the moment, there are more than six thousand newsgroups online with an estimated 3 to 4 million Usenet users. Perhaps this popularity can be explained by the way that Usenet accommodates such a diversity of topics and individuals, containing groups as different as **alt.fan.rush-limbaugh, alt.sex.spanking, k12.ed.science, misc. activism.progressive** and **soc.culture.kurdish.**

Newsgroups can be directed at audiences ranging from the local to the international. Many academic institutions, for example, will offer newsgroup services for affiliated courses and individuals. Most groups, however, are global in scope. For the purposes of our discussion, we divide groups roughly into three categories: news feeds, moderated groups, and unmoderated groups.

- **News feeds** represent the most familiar form of newsgroup information. Groups based on news feeds collect traditional news from wire services like the Associated Press and Reuters. Usually listed under the large CATEGORY or "Clari" newsgroups, these groups can be extremely useful for students doing basic research, providing instant access to a wide variety of current resources. Check with your instructor about the availability of the Clari news feeds at your institution.

- **Moderated groups** operate on the premise that messages posted to the group should be filtered through a moderator; therefore, not every message sent to a moderated list will be posted. Because messages which lean toward unsubstantiated personal rants are generally censored, postings to a moderated list often fall into the category of expert opinions or topic-centered articles. Many of these posts can be well argued and offer fairly knowledgeable insight into a research topic.

- **Unmoderated groups** are open to anyone and offer the best opportunity for viewing the diverse types of written interaction that can take place on Usenet newsgroups. Messages display varying levels of formality (ranging between scholarly articles and "chat") and often prompt substantial interaction. A posted message and subsequent responses (composing a *thread*) reveal a dialogue that often moves between a series of arguments and counter-arguments.

While these categories represent useful distinctions, most newsgroup discussions are unmoderated and involve a range of activities and types of messages. In some ways, the messages found on a newsgroup can be compared to those shared via a Listserv (see Chapter 2). The postings generally relate to a single topic and often provide insight and perspectives from knowledgeable individuals that can be easily incorporated as resources for student compositions. Some groups are more directly analogous to traditional print media, while others range toward personal opinion.

Although the audiences for newsgroup postings are quite broad, they are limited in other ways, primarily by the topic of each of the newsgroups. On an active group, the feedback that you may receive comes from informed readers who are knowledgeable about their subject matter—particularly beneficial when you are writing a research paper outside of your instructor's area of expertise. It can be helpful to post messages early in your research process to ask advice about sources or to get feedback about your ideas as they begin to take shape.

While individual newsgroups are limited in scope, with a substantial depth of topic in each, keep in mind that newsgroups in general are limited as a resource in other ways. While many knowledgeable Internet users can provide source information for an unlimited number of issues, overall the Internet underrepresents certain minority groups, economic classes and even entire continents. Further, the English language dominates the Internet, and there are only a few non-English speaking newsgroups. Remember that newsgroup audiences may have important gaps in their demographic makeup which will necessarily have effects on the kind of information the Internet gives you.

MINING THE COMMUNAL RESOURCE

Newsgroups closely intertwine the processes of research and conversation. You may begin using a newsgroup by gleaning information from it, but soon may post queries for further information, or participate actively in the group's ongoing discussion. If you use the discussion to clarify points about your topic, then the conversation itself can serve as a means of research.

Perhaps the greatest benefit of researching with newsgroups is their currency. One type of group offers news feeds from wire services like the Associated Press and Reuters, providing materials that appear in newspapers around the country. News is thus available as immediately as in a newspaper or on television, with the additional strength of near comprehensive coverage: anything the wire services produce is available online, whereas any particular newspaper has to curtail radically the amount of material it is able to present.

Full Group List

	Third World Newsgroups
alt.creative.c	
alt.cuddle	
alt.cult-movie	6289 alt.activism
alt.cult-movie	491 alt.activism.d
alt.cult-movie	17 alt.culture.somalia
alt.culture.a	alt.culture.tamil
alt.culture.ar	5 alt.culture.southasianet
alt.culture.au	66 clari.news.poverty
alt.culture.be	322 clari.news.terrorism
alt.culture.bu	448 clari.news.usa.gov.foreign_policy
alt.culture.cc	548 clari.world.africa
alt.culture.eg	87 clari.world.africa.south_africa
alt.culture.el	clari.world.americas
alt.culture.hc	108 clari.world.americas.caribbean
alt.culture.ir	48 clari.world.americas.central
alt.culture.ir	86 clari.world.americas.mexico
alt.culture.kc	268 clari.world.americas.south
alt.culture.ke	clari.world.asia
alt.culture.ku	72 clari.world.asia.central
alt.culture.mi	192 clari.world.asia.india
alt.culture.ne	204 clari.world.asia.south
alt.culture.nu	567 clari.world.asia.southeast
alt.culture.or	124 clari.world.mideast.iran
alt.culture.ri	27 clari.world.mideast.iraq
alt.culture.sc	352 misc.activism.progressive
alt.culture.sc	34 clari.world.mideast.turkey
alt.culture.sc	9999 soc.culture.indian
alt.culture.tc	5 soc.culture.indian.info

Although we have outlined distinctions between news feeds, moderated groups, and unmoderated groups, it can be more helpful to focus on the groups' messages and conversations. Besides news feeds, newsgroups fall roughly into two categories: "serious" and "chat." The serious groups, moderated or unmoderated, are more analytical and present a wider variety of opinions than the news feeds. Participants in these groups are often experts, and their opinions may be based on scholarly research of their own.

One benefit of serious newsgroups is that they offer significant information that is often absent from mainstream news sources, especially concerning international and Third World issues. For example, along with international news feeds on the January 1994 uprising in Chiapas, Mexico, newsgroups have provided the text of political pamphlets from the region. Thus current, locally produced information (unfiltered by publishers) becomes available to interested readers around the world.

The "chat" groups are less useful for serious researchers. Social message boards focusing on nonacademic subjects, groups like **alt.sex. stories, alt.alien.vampire.flonk.flonk.flonk,** and **rec.games.video. arcade** will probably not be appropriate for your research project. Some "chat" groups can be useful, however. For example, the conversation on **alt.fan.tarantino** would prove interesting if your research paper considered the film *Reservoir Dogs.*

READING CRITICALLY

The volume of information available on newsgroups demands evaluation and critical reading skills. Because of the comparative absence of filtering processes like those more broadly employed in print publication, excellent materials are "published" on Usenet which would otherwise find space only in low-circulation, local presses, if anywhere. At the same time, because anyone with access to the Internet can post information and arguments to newsgroups, the material can often be untrustworthy.

Newsgroups are a paradox—a source of information both less reliable and more reliable than familiar items such as magazine articles. They may be less reliable because it is as easy to post (and thus "publish") off-hand messages with mistaken information as it is to post well-considered messages with viable arguments and accurate information. Because the thoughtful and thoughtless messages appear side by side and in the same format, you need to distinguish potentially problematic messages from the two other broad categories of messages discussed above: postings from news feeds and messages from the "serious," more analytical discussion groups (which often make use of detailed research).

What is significant about Usenet is that most groups make little distinction among all these various types of messages. As a result, many newsgroups take on a kind of editorial objectivity which is quite different from that surrounding the printed source. When you read a magazine, for instance, you may notice that less "authoritative" material such as a letter to the editor is separated from the featured articles. Furthermore, you won't be able to see the many articles that were not selected for publication by the editors. In contrast, when you enter a thread of discussion in a newsgroup, you are instantly surrounded by a number of divergent voices and opinions, all pulling against one another in a variety of ways. Through a careful process of critical reading, you might actually come to a fuller sense of the complexity of an issue than you might reach after reading isolated printed sources. The printed text by its very singular authority often cannot acknowledge the full range of other positions and voices that surround it in a public debate. Reading newsgroups, you may come to appreciate the extent to which both experts and hacks help define the terminology of a debate, its boundaries, its stakes.

A THREAD DISCUSSING HEALTH CARE IN *ALT.ACTIVISM*

-		William Wallis	Re: More news on Foster -- almost buried
-		Children Now	Chidren Now: New Web Site
▽	7	Jim Nakamura	Re: What Happened to Health Care
		Donna Kinney	Re: What Happened to Health Care
		Karl Dussik	Re: What Happened to Health Care
		Jim Nakamura	Re: What Happened to Health Care
		Jim Nakamura	Re: What Happened to Health Care
		Sandy	Re: What Happened to Health Care
		ir000212@interra	Re: What Happened to Health Care
-		Jon Roland	Re: REPORT: A.D.L. of B'nai B'rith Linke
▷	2	Pete Zakel	Re: MEDICAL POT MEANS POT FOR ALL
-		Kevin Darcy	Re: What will support@netcom.com do now?
▷	4	Ted Krueger	Re: Ok, but what about regulation? (was

In general, newsgroups facilitate the process of gathering various perspectives on the same issue. Messages found within the same thread often comment on, critique, or revise previous messages. The thread presents rich material demanding critical reading—that is, granting the writer as much credibility as possible while simultaneously keeping in mind opposing points of view and possible points of rebuttal. By looking at an entire thread in a newsgroup instead of a single article on an issue, or two pieces which oppose one another, you find how many positions and assumptions are open to refutation.

POSTING AND GATHERING

With literally thousands of different Usenet groups to choose from, there is an excellent chance that you will discover groups discussing issues important to you and/or useful for researching class projects. At the same time, however, the overwhelming list of groups can be disorienting, and the process of searching through thousands of prefixed and suffixed names can be frustrating and time-consuming. Your instructor may have developed a list of relevant groups on the system's news reader, so you can scan the full list and select a few that seem most closely related to your topic and interests. While you are scanning, notice the range of different groups and types of conversation available in Usenet news.

Get accustomed to the idea of browsing newsgroups as a means of gathering materials for your research papers and projects. There are a number of topics for which Usenet will offer more (and more significant) materials than a traditional library. If you use Usenet groups to research extremely current topics, or topics which are particularly heavily discussed online—current Third World issues, environmental concerns, computer or technology topics—you will very likely find much more material than you would searching through a library's collection of books and periodicals.

Also remember that newsgroups offer an extremely broad array of materials. You will be able to find not only well-written articles, but also important documents (for example, government legislation or official UN statements), as well as an array of opinions and perspectives on the issue. As we suggested above, this variety of information and multiplicity of voices can be addressed through a careful process of critical reading.

Keep in mind that newsgroups, by their very nature, are geared toward current events. Since the groups have limited storage size, newer postings displace older ones after a certain amount of time, or after the group has exceeded its size limitations. For researchers this means that the content of the groups is constantly changing, and a post that is available one week may be gone the next (especially on groups with heavy traffic). Unless you record them, resources can disappear from the group before you have a chance to get needed statistics or citation information. For this reason, always save and document any posts that you find particularly useful. If you are not sure what exactly you will need, it is always better to keep too much source information than not enough. It is a good idea to reserve a diskette solely for newsgroup resources. If you are using client software, you can archive the material you find online and "cut and paste" quotations into your papers once you have begun writing.

Additionally, we encourage you to use the interactive capabilities of newsgroups. Beyond just mining Usenet for existing resources, consider posting questions and requests for information about your topic to appropriate newsgroups. Usenet provides a tremendous amount of expertise on even the most obscure topics. Of course, the people reading and writing these groups are not librarians paid to answer questions—they participate in the discussions for their own benefit and enjoyment. Group members will resent feeling obligated to answer obvious factual or historical questions. That is why it is crucial to spend time familiarizing yourself with the key issues, terms, and players in a debate before posting questions to group.

This is not to say that the newsgroup audience is unwilling to offer assistance. In fact, participants are surprisingly helpful and will often write long and thoughtful replies to student requests. In order to receive this help, though, you will need to compose your questions carefully. A confident but polite tone will go a long way towards eliciting useful feedback, but will not make up for a poorly conceived message. Do not generalize when composing questions, but rather be specific about what you already know on the topic, and what you need to know. Be careful with your use of important terms—the difference between "Croat" and "Croatian," for example, may be extremely crucial to some participants in a discussion about conflict in the former Yugoslavia. The best questions will spark debate on the newsgroup and allow the group members to offer assistance to the student while maintaining their existing level of conversation.

CHAPTER 4

*Real-Time Discussion: IRC and MU*s*

WHAT IS INTERNET RELAY CHAT (IRC)?

Internet Relay Chat (IRC) allows communication over the Internet as if in a conference call or over a CB radio channel. Using IRC, users can participate in topic-centered, real-time discussions over channels (or lines) that are roughly equivalent to radio frequencies.

Like the Usenet groups discussed in the previous chapter, the channels of IRC center on specific topics. In IRC channels, however, users can do more than participate on an existing channel; they can also quickly create their own channels. What makes IRC interesting is that multiple users around the globe can communicate in real-time with only a slight lag between exchanges. This almost instantaneous transfer of messages in IRC allows users to communicate in a way that resembles face-to-face conversation. Unlike e-mail or newsgroups, which are "asynchronous" (i.e., there is an expected delay between messages) IRC lines allow for synchronous conversation.

This immediacy can present a problem though; if your audience is not physically present, how can you convey the sorts of nonverbal signals (expressions, gestures, tone of voice, etc.) that people use in conversation? IRC allows users to send these signals with commands that represent the signal as something other than speech. Characters can uses emotes, or descriptions of actions they are virtually "performing." For example, a user named Socrates could type *:listens intently.* and the text transmitted to other participants would read *Socrates listens intently.* In this way users can interact through writing—not only with conversational dialogue, but also by describing that dialogue.

A helpful way of looking at real-time discussions is as a hybrid that blends elements of writing and speech. A discussion in IRC reads a little like a manuscript of a play, in which a scrolling screen displays participants' names followed by a colon and then their dialogue or emotes. This sense of the theatrical is compounded by the fact that users are referred to as characters and they often take on pseudonyms while online.

WHAT ARE MU*S?

Like the IRC channels, MU*s offer spaces in which real-time written conversation and interaction can take place. MU* indicates a certain type of text-based, virtual environment, the first of which were the Multi User Domains (or "Dungeons"). MUDs were initially designed as a more sophisticated medium in which to engage in role-playing games like Dungeons and Dragons. Rather than use graphics to represent the fantastic worlds of these games, MUD participants could construct complex environments out of descriptive passages of text. These descriptions were placed on the Internet and scripted in a way which allowed multiple users to log on and be simultaneously present in the virtual space, adding an important interactive element to the games. Until recently these spaces have existed mainly as a forum for social interaction and gamesmanship. During the last few years, however, academics have started to see the value of these text-based environments and have begun to apply them to any number of scholarly projects.

MUDs gave birth to numerous different formats with names like MUSH and Tiny MUSH, each of which has slightly different protocols and scripting languages, as well as to the "MUD Object Oriented," or MOO. Rather than try to distinguish between MUDs, MUSHes, MOOs, and a host of other acronyms, we will use the term MU* to indicate a variety of these text-based virtual spaces. Because of the growing tendency for the more "academically oriented" of these spaces to be constructed using MOO scripts, we will provide examples mainly about MOO commands. Those details which do apply specifically to MOOs, however, can almost always be adapted with only minor variations to the other MU* formats.

Unlike the IRCs, the space of a MU* is a highly circumscribed environment in which the surroundings will dictate many of the user's options. Within the same MU*, a user could easily wander into and out of the reference section of a university library, a public hearing in a fourth century BCE Grecian polis, a sci-fi nightmare, the second act of a Beckett play, the set of a movie, or just about anywhere else that someone might have imagined—all mapped out through textual descriptions. Rather than simply reading through the scrolling dialogue of an IRC channel, MU* users can move around, look at objects, and engage with their environment on a number of other levels.

MU*s and IRCs also free the class from some of the logistical constraints of the traditional classroom. A class that wanted to meet with students from another section or from another institution could log on to a MU* or an IRC environment. Similarly, an instructor could arrange to bring a number of guests from remote locations into the "classroom," or send students into MU*s and IRCs that are frequented by people outside of the class itself. As we have discussed in previous chapters, this kind of interaction with an expanded audience presents an important challenge to writers. You must shape your messages for your readership, and be prepared to receive engaging and sometimes challenging response and feedback.

IRC CHANNELS AND ONLINE DISCUSSION

Accessing and participating in IRC is a fairly simple procedure. If you are connected directly to a Unix-based network at your institution, for example, you might simply type "irc" to connect to the IRC server. Often, however, you will use an IRC client program on your workstation, which provides a much easier interface for your IRC sessions. Some common IRC clients are IRCle (for Macintosh) and MIRC (for Windows). These client programs will have the locations of IRC servers—often more than a hundred—pre-scripted for easy access. If you have been given instructions to connect to a specific IRC server, you can do so easily within the IRC client program. If not, you can experiment with different servers to see the types of channels that are available on each.

Once you are connected to IRC, you will need to distinguish between commands that you issue to the IRC server and the words that you wish to communicate to the group. The first character of a command is always slash (/). Some of the basic commands allow you to list or join channels or modify your nickname. Because the IRC clients facilitate conversation, simply typing a line of text and pressing "enter" will send the message to all the users currently subscribed on an IRC channel. Your nickname will be attached to the text you write so that the message will automatically be ascribed to you. Thus, after a very brief introduction to the technology, you will find that the operation of IRC discussion is, for the most part, removed to the background.

IRC commands

- /join #*rhetoric*
  Joins you to an existing channel (here, #rhetoric): if the channel doesn't exist, it will be created as a new channel
- /list
  Lists all currently available channels. Be aware, though, that since there are often thousands of channels available on a single server, listing them all will tie up your machine for several minutes. Type "/help /list" once you are online to manage this list.
- /nick *newnickname*
  Changes your nickname to whatever you type in place of "newnickname."
- /names
  Shows nicknames of users on each channel.

29

- /who *channel*
  Shows who is on a given channel.
- /whois *nick*
  Shows "true" identity of someone on a channel.

To create a new IRC channel, you simply join a channel that doesn't already exist. Choose a name obscure enough that it won't already be in use, but clear enough that the people you want to participate will recognize it.

SPEAKING, EMOTING, NAVIGATING, AND BUILDING WITH A MU*

While MU*s offer a greater range of interactivity than the chat channels of IRC, they also require more time for learning the fundamentals of the medium.

As with e-mail and newsgroups, you can get to a MU* with a simple Telnet connection; this is the most basic way to connect to a server. Enter the IP address followed by the port number (usually either 7777 or 8888). For example, the address of Diversity University MOO is **moo.du.org 8888**. The interface provided by this kind of connection, however, is a bit cumbersome. For instance, the other users will scroll onto the screen as you compose new messages, breaking up the text you are trying to enter.

MU*s can also be accessed by activating a client application which resides on a remote machine. Though these programs still rely on a Telnet connection, their interface allows a user to compose more easily and keep a record of the MU* session. Their operation may require knowledge of specialized commands.

Workstation client applications, such as MUDDweller or Mudling (for Macintosh) or MUTT or MudWin (for Windows), available by FTP as freeware, are the easiest way to log on to a MU*. Programs like this assist navigation, offer separate windows for composing messages, and provide easily retrievable transcripts. The simple connection and the rapid transfer of text are two reasons that MU*s have become so popular.

Many MU*s offer individual accounts to regular visitors with personalized names and passwords, and most MU*s have easy-to-use anonymous logins that allow first-time or infrequent users access to the

30

MU*. If you plan to add any rooms or other features to the structure of a MU*, you will probably need to have an individual account on the server, and permission from its system administrators.

Although some MU*s will require guests to use prefabricated identities, most will allow new users to configure temporary names and descriptions for their characters. By typing the command *@desc me as a broad-shouldered guy carrying a Frisbee* a user named "bozo" would set his character description. Any other user who typed *look bozo* would see "a broad-shouldered guy carrying a Frisbee." You should take some time to construct a description of yourself as you wish to be seen. Define the gender of a character by typing *@gender* followed by *male, female,* or *neuter*; this will configure the gender of your persona with one of the traditional set of gender pronouns. You can usually see the full range of gender options on a MU* by typing *@gender* by itself. Daedalus MOO, for example, lets the user choose from a number of options: either (s/he), egotistical (I), plural (they), royal (we), splat (*e,h*), or even Spivak (e, em, eir, eirs, eirself, E, Em, Eir, Eirs, Eirself).

While we've talked about the ways that MU*s and IRCs challenge the idea of authorship through their electronic mesages, we don't want to suggest that they make a writer completely anonymous. In fact, one of the values of using IRCs, and probably to a larger extent MU*s, is that they allow students to develop alternative identities. You can experiment with online constructions of identity, as well as study audience reaction to various personas. For instance, the appearance of "an elderly, well-dressed African-American woman who would look equally comfortable lecturing in a university or serving food to the homeless with Food Not Bombs" is almost certain to change the flow of a conversation about affirmative action in institutions of higher learning.

The primary interaction that takes place on a MU* is text-based communication. The basic commands are *say* and *emote* (though these can usually be shortened to " and : respectively). The *say* command (") attributes your name to any message you want to send. For example if your user name is "Athena" and you type in the line *Nobody knows you're a god on the Internet.*, everyone in the room (including you) will see the message *Athena says, "Nobody knows you're a god on the Internet."* The *say* command simply tells the MU* server to place your username and the word "says" in front of exactly what you type.

Similarly, the *emote* command (:) is used to attribute actions to you. It places your name in front of the text you type after the command. For example, the line *:rises in splendor and heads for the nearest temple.* will return the message *Athena rises in splendor and heads for the nearest temple.*

31

Though all interaction is thus narrated in third person, it is possible to communicate a wide range of thoughts, emotions, and actions Since whatever you type after a say or emote command appears on the screen, you can include any number of sentences or any symbol you wish. The most obvious use of this feature is to "say" things with the *emote* command. By typing a message like *:says painfully, "I didn't know that was going to happen."* you will produce *Athena says painfully, "I didn't know that was going to happen."*

Emoting allows expression of any number of different attitudes, for instance humor or irony. To express certain subtle feelings, however, you must communicate through your writing rather than through emotes.

The basic MU* navigation commands are simply north, south, east, and west, but rooms in MU*s are often built to offer other dimensions of motion. A well-constructed room will inform a user about the possible options for movement and investigation. In fact the details of a MU* environment can be quite elaborate and creative. Thus, building spaces on a MU* can require creative writing skills unlike those of the prose that may be stressed in the classroom. The well-worn dictum that descriptive writers should "show not tell" is especially pertinent for MU* environments. The skills you gain from writing precise descriptive prose for a MU* can be usefully extended to the explications that you make in all your wiiting.

Basic MOO commands

x is a variable which stands for information
you must enter with the command

look *x* — provides a description of the current room unless an object is specified

" *x* — allows you to "say" whatever you type in after the command

: *x* — makes your character "emote" whatever you type after the command

whisper "x**" to** *c* — speaks the message *x* only to the designated character *c*

read *x* — use to "read" newspapers or signs MOOs

@desc me as *x* — provides a descriptio: *x* of yourself for those who "look" at you

@gender *x* — gives your character t gender *x*

@help or help — gives more detailed information about MOO commands and their syntax

32

@dig "[new-room-name]"	creates a room	**@nogo**	what you see if you can't go through an exit
@desc [object] as "[description]"	describes a room or an object	**@onogo**	what others see if you can't go through an exit
@add-exit	creates an exit		
@add-entrance	creates an entrance	**@create [object type] named "[name]"**	creates a new object of a given type ($note, $letter, $thing, or $container)
@dig [direction] to "[room]"	links an exit and an entrance		
@leave	defines what you see just before you go through an exit		
		@take	picks up an object
@oleave	what others see when you leave	**@take_succeeded**	what you see when you take
@arrive	what you see after you arrive in a room	**@otake_succeeded**	what others see when you take
@oarrive	what others see when you arrive in a room	**@take_failed**	what you see if you can't take
		@otake_failed	what others see if you can't take
@lock	prevents other users from entering a room or taking an object	**@drop**	drops an object

@drop_succeeded   what you
               see when you
               drop

@odrop_succeeded
               what others
               see when you
               drop

@drop_failed   what you see
               when you
               can't drop

@odrop_failed   what others
               see when you
               can't drop

CHAPTER 5

The Electronic Library: Browsing with Gopher and the World Wide Web

In order to select and incorporate successfully the seemingly limitless resources that are available on the Internet (the "information superhighway"), students need to learn effective online research strategies. Though we call this process of researching with the Internet *browsing*, the term encompasses more than the traditional notion of walking through a section of the library and choosing books off the shelf. While browsing the Internet, a user connects to different sites around the world, actively explores directories of information, performs automated keyword searches of multiple files, and downloads and saves any useful resources (including graphic, sound, and video files).

GOPHER

Browsing on the Internet was first made possible by *Gopher*, a system of Internet protocols and directory structures that allows users to reach different machines worldwide and to view and search directory structures and available files. Along with a new ability to move fluidly from one site to another, Gopher provided a more user-friendly interface for file transfer protocol (FTP), the system that allows files to move from one site to another (see Chapter 1). Through Gopher, a user could for the first time easily browse the contents of Internet hosts and retrieve the files stored there. Computer science departments, libraries, and whole institutions quickly adopted this medium as a way to disseminate and share information. While in the last two years, use of the World Wide Web has almost fully supplanted Gopher, researchers at some institutions may still make use of the technology.

A Gopher server (also referred to as a Gopherhost) stores and hierarchically organizes information which is read via a Gopher client application. A menu-driven Gopher interface (but without mouse support) can be accessed from most servers, with client software which operates from the server; on a Unix-based server, for example, this is done simply by typing *gopher* and the address of a host. With Gopher, these server-based client applications are fairly effective. A user will generally select items from a menu by entering the number that corresponds to the function they wish to perform.

A Gopher client residing on a workstation, however, provides a much easier interface for searching and accessing documents and directories in *Gopherspace* (the universe of files accessible by Gopher clients). A file or application retrieved from a remote host is said to be *downloaded*.

Along with an easy interface, workstation Gopher clients offer several other advantages. A user can create *bookmarks*, electronic pointers to a Gopher site that can be recalled for future reference. A list of bookmarks is known as a *hotlist*. Users can also save text files, download and open graphic or sound files, and record a history of the files and directories that have been accessed since turning on the Gopher client.

Although Gopher functions have changed somewhat (especially with the ongoing absorption of Gopherspace by the World Wide Web), there are still three primary strategies for finding specific information using Gopher:

- **Targeting.** The user connects directly to a known address at a specific machine (a *Gopherhost*) and hunts through the site.
- **Tunneling.** The user accesses a number of Gopherhosts and explores their directories, which are organized both geographically as well as by subject. For instance, a user who was looking for information at MIT could follow the path "World/North America/United States/Massachusetts/MIT." The same user could search for information by subject, beginning in broadly-defined directories such as "Libraries," "Government," or "Jobs." Since Gopher sites are organized hierarchically (much like the directory or folder structure of most personal computer operating systems), they can contribute structure to the wealth of information on the Internet. Each Gopher server organizes only the material on that local site, although researchers will become familiar with similar patterns of organization throughout Gopherspace. A user can move up or down through a Gopher site with some sense of direction.
- **Keyword Searching.** The user can use special functions of the Gopher client to search Gopherspace and retrieve files or directories containing specified words.

THE WORLD WIDE WEB

The World Wide Web (also known as *WWW* or *the Web*) is a communication system built on the Internet's global network of computer networks that presents information in a variety of media in a richly interconnected way. The Web was built upon older protocols (FTP, Gopher, etc.) and additional newer protocols, such as Hypertext Transfer Protocol (HTTP). Client software called *Web browsers* allow the user to view many types of files (HTML, GIF, text, etc.), as well as navigate among files. Each file on the World Wide Web is assigned an address called a *Uniform Resource Locator (URL)*, which tells the browser the exact location of the file. Files are stored on Web servers which are equipped with software that enables documents to be linked and shared.

If the only Internet technology you have access to is Telnet, you may still be able to reach World Wide Web files. Web clients can reside on remote computers and can be accessed with a simple Telnet connection. Here, for example is the interface for Lynx, a Unix-based text-only Web browser:

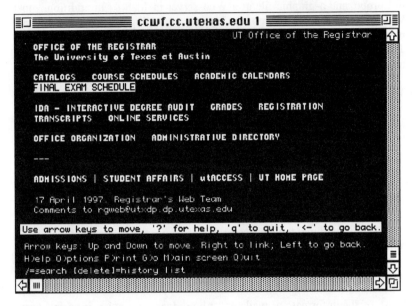

Each of the capitalized words or phrases is a *link*; links are followed using the arrow-keys, and other single keystroke options are available. Because Web pages contain multimedia elements, these Telnet connections give you severely limited access to the Web.

Of all the client software, workstation Web browsers are the most essential for taking full advantage of the capabilities of the Internet. Web browsers have subsumed some of the functions of e-mail, newsgroups, Gopher, Telnet, and FTP. In addition, these clients seamlessly weave together the multimedia resources of the Web. Besides offering navigational aids like bookmarks or hotlists, Web browsers offer a number of other features.

Browsing the World Wide Web, like searching with Gopher, allows users to access and download files at a site, examine and explore broad topic categories, and perform a multitude of keyword searches. However, unlike Gopher, where a user will tunnel up or down among hierarchies, the hypertextual capabilities of the Web allow connections between documents regardless of their location. A single Web page can display multimedia files and link to other documents on local or remote servers. A page might link to a sound file at an FTP site in Australia, a text file at a Gopher site in Europe, and a graphic file at a Web server in Idaho. In addition, most Web browsers now incorporate Internet technologies, like Gopher and newsgroups, which previously demanded their own client applications. The connectivity and multimedia possibilities of the Web have greatly helped the recent growth of the Internet.

The remainder of this chapter will discuss in more detail the value of browsing the Internet for student research. It will also offer some helpful advice on browsing strategies and conclude with a sample browsing session illustrating the narrowing of a research topic and the gathering of Internet resources.

RESEARCH, DISCOVERY, AND ANALYSIS

Browsing is a crucial tool for research. It uncovers excellent material on an unlimited range of subjects. It can teach valuable research skills, such as narrowing a topic, evaluating source material, and incorporating online research effectively into your writing.

Most of the information available online does not exist in print form. Browsing on the Internet, researchers will likely find electronic journals, online reference materials like encyclopedias, archives of newsgroup or Listserv postings, institutional publications (academic, corporate, nonprofit, etc.), personal commentary, and other forms of electronic conversation. In certain areas—Third World news, computer information, environmental issues, political discussion, and many others—the Net offers unparalleled resources. More and more, institutions are using the Web as a storehouse for official documents of all types and for information about extremely current events.

While there is an incredible volume and range of resource material available online, researching on the Internet can be difficult. First, online information exists on different servers all over the world, and although this information may be organized locally, nowhere is there a comprehensive list of available resources. Second, material on the Internet is often short-lived. As servers are reorganized, site addresses are changed, and documents are replaced, information available one day can be gone the next. Additionally, because of the tremendous growth of the Internet, and especially the Web, new information is being added constantly. Successive searches will often produce different results as new documents come online, so that its difficult to conduct truly comprehensive research.

Despite these and other challenges of online research, the fundamental techniques involved in using the Internet as a research tool are quite similar to library research skills. Topics still have to be narrowed, searches refined, and source materials evaluated.

Incorporating browsing in the stages of research

Finding a topic Tunnel through Gopherspace, surf the Web, or perform keyword searches as you brainstorm on possible topics.

Narrowing and refining the topic Once a broad topic has been settled upon, run a more extensive set of keyword searches can help (see the Case Study below for an extended example of this process).

Finding and evaluating sources When you have settled on a suitable topic, review the Gopher and Web sites you visited while refining the topic. Determine whether they now offer new information or links, and investigate any promising new links. Perform additional key word searches relating to all aspects of your project. Look for sites that refer to your sources (both online and other) to see what others have said about them.

The enormous volume of material that browsing usually yields makes evaluating source material critical. As is the case when using most Internet research tools, browsing Gopherspace and the Web will generally turn up a wide range of information— in terms of both quantity and quality. Researchers investigating human rights abuses in East Timor, for example, will likely need to balance the various authorities of material published by government organizations like the CIA, nongovernmental organizations like Amnesty International, corporate organizations like CitiBank who wish to invest in the region, academic observers like Noam Chomsky, and a host of individuals who may have collected information and "published" their opinions about the situation. Selecting from this range of sources, researchers often find themselves in the position of weighing a well-written, well-researched article taken from a Gopher site (and therefore displayed in unattractive, unformatted ASCII text), against information that may be less relevant but that comes from a well-designed Web site complete with stylish text layout, graphics, video, and sound. In many cases, multimedia elements add immensely to an audience's understanding of a particular topic, but students should not overlook authoritative material which comes in visually less engaging formats.

TARGETING A SPECIFIC SITE

As we suggested earlier in this chapter, our concept of "browsing" includes both Gopher and the World Wide Web. As we also mentioned earlier in this chapter, strategies for browsing (whether through Gopher or the Web) fall into three broad categories: connecting directly to a known site (targeting), following paths and links to search for materials (tunneling or surfing), and making use of keyword searches.

While the software you use to browse Gopherspace will probably be configured to use your school's host, you will be able to begin another Gopher session by entering an alternate Gopher address. Gopherhost addresses are machine names; therefore, they look much like the portion of an e-mail address following the @ symbol. For instance, you might connect directly to the host *Gopher2.tc.umn.edu* at the University of Minnesota, where Gopher was first developed.

If you already know the location of a site, you can search it out by moving through a sequence of geographical hierarchies. For example, say that you wanted to connect to the Gopher archive called the Latin America Network Information Center (sponsored by the Institute for Latin American Studies at the University of Texas). You would most likely select a directory called "World," after which you would move through a series of progressively narrower hierarchies. From the "World" directory you would first choose "North America," then "United States," then "Texas," then "University of Texas at Austin." You would then choose "Colleges and Departments," then "College of Liberal Arts," then "LANIC." Note also that once you have located a useful site, using the bookmark feature of your client software can allow you to jump directly to that spot without having to follow the full path again. Although this process involves the techniques of tunneling, we include it in the discussion of targeting because the user is trying to reach a specific destination. For those who cannot enter a Gopherhost address directly, this method of targeting is the easiest way to locate a particular Gopher site.

When using the Web, the strategy of targeting becomes much more important for the simple reason that each file has its own specific address or URL (for more on URLs, see pp. 57-58). Since the Web is not organized in clear hierarchical directories, following paths to specific sites or documents can be quite difficult. For this reason targeting is a primary means of locating information; at any point a user can enter a URL and connect directly to a desired page or file. Since locating a site often depends on knowing its address, URLs are frequently distributed on e-mail Listservs and newsgroups in order to publicize the sites to interested audiences.

TUNNELING GOPHERS AND WEB SURFERS

Subject directories or "trees" are a good starting point for students who have a broad idea of their topic but do not yet have a keyword narrow enough to bring back a manageable amount of material (see "Keyword Searches" below). The trick is finding a good set of subject headings. If your school provides its own Gopherhost, check there first to see what subject categories are available to you. If not, you might try initiating your research from a well-established site like the University of Minnesota. Since seeking out a good subject tree on another Gopher host can be rather difficult, and since subject trees in Gopher are generally not very well developed, we also suggest exploring a World Wide Web research tool (such as Yahoo, ElNet Galaxy, or Infoseek), which abound with complex subject directories that can lead you to useful resources. While search engines for other protocols (such as Veronica and WAIS) can also be helpful, Web keyword search engines examine a much broader field of information.

Ironically, although the Web provides a more useful set of subject headings than Gopher does, the Web often replaces the hierarchical, vertical model of "tunneling" with the less structured metaphor of "surfing," or navigating from site to site in a nonlinear and nonhierarchical manner. While the designers of many Web research tools have made use of subject trees, the Web itself is not hierarchical, as is the directory and file structure of Gopher. The hypertextual capabilities of the Web allow creators of home pages to provide links to related material, which in turn have links to further material, and so on in a never-ending Web of connections. Because the paths you take while surfing the Web may be difficult to replicate, you should make use of bookmarks to note the location of sites you find useful.

KEYWORD SEARCHES

BOOLEAN OPERATORS

Most of the engines for keyword searches use some form of Boolean operators to modify search strings. Employing these commands allows the user to narrow a search and to bring back a smaller number of "hits." We list some of the basic commands here, with which you may be familiar from searching various library databases (such as the MLA online index).

Entering	Searches for
term1 term2 term3	all occurrences of either term1 or term2 or term3
term1 AND term2	only occurrences of both terms 1 and 2

term1 OR term2	either term1 or term2
term1 NOT term2	only occurrences of term1 which do not contain term2
term1*	occurrences of the root within other words (a "Fuzzy Search" of term1)
"term1 term2 term3"	only occurrences of all three terms together (a "Literal Search")

The terms can also be used in conjunction with one another. For example, the search pattern

racial OR sexual AND discrimination OR bias

would produce a series of hits containing any combination of the following phrases: racial discrimination, sexual discrimination, racial bias, sexual bias (but not occurrences of only one of the terms on its own).

Not every search engine uses Boolean operators in exactly the same way. Check the information provided at the site of the search engine to find out which functions are supported.

WAIS

WAIS, the Wide Area Information Search, is a powerful tool that helps users locate and extract information from a collection of documents. It is a long-standing public domain search engine, whose name is now something of a misnomer. The search covers a "wide area" in that it allows you to search multiple databases, but its area of coverage is narrower than more recently developed tools (like Veronica) that search multiple hosts worldwide. WAIS searches only a limited number of databases and requires that certain connections be established between the WAIS software and the text to be searched. WAIS searches are employed on Gopher sites, on Web sites, and on local databases.

Although (or perhaps because) WAIS covers a narrower body of materials than other searches, some of its search capabilities are more powerful. Many WAIS hosts will allow you to search the complete text of documents for your keywords, instead of just their titles or subject lines (as Veronica does, for example). Most WAIS applications support Boolean search strings, which will constitute the primary method for you to narrow your searches. For more information about the capabilities of WAIS and the material it covers at a particular site, look for a "readme" or FAQ file located on the site.

VERONICA

Veronica is an index and retrieval system that can locate items on 99 percent of the Gopher servers around the world. As of January 1995 (the most recent figures available), the Veronica index contained about 15 million items from approximately fifteen thousand servers.

To initiate a Veronica search, you must first connect to a site (located in cities like New York, Pisa, Cologne, and Bergen) that offers the service. Because such servers are often flooded with other users, a good strategy for trying to connect is to choose a host located in a part of the world where it is currently the middle of the night and fewer local users are likely to be logged on. Increasingly, however, even this strategy will not help. Some Gopherhosts now automate the login process, connecting you to the host with the least amount of traffic at the time of your request.

Once you log on to a Veronica host, you will be asked to enter a search string. Note that Veronica searches for words in titles of sources; it does not perform a full-text search of the contents of the sources.

If a Veronica search returns few or no sources, you can broaden the search without changing keywords. Veronica makes use of the asterisk wildcard; using it tells the computer to search for all occurrences of the root within other words (but the asterisk can only be used at the end of the root, not at the beginning or in the middle). This can be especially helpful, since the titles of Gopher files are often abbreviated to save space. A search for *envir** will turn up not only titles using environment, environmental, environmentalism, and so on, but also a file named *environ.amazon.txt*.

If you are searching Veronica for a specific type of source, like image or text files, use the *-t* command followed by a number or letter for the source type. Some of the official file types include *O* (text files), *s* (sound files), *g* (GIF image files), and *I* (image files in formats other than GIF). For example, if you wanted to search for image files relating to George Washington, you would enter *George Washington-tI*. (When typing commands, leave no spaces between the items.) For further information about using these additional Veronica search commands, look for a "readme" or FAQ file in the search directory.

A Veronica search will produce a list of items very similar to WAIS results. The primary difference is that the items contained in it point to sites all over the world rather than reside on the same host. Research can thus be compounded by certain problems. With the duplication of materials on the Internet, different listings might actually take the user to the same resource, stored on two or more different sites. Additionally, certain sites may temporarily be down or too busy to allow connections. For these reasons, you should save the search results as a file so that you can return to those sites when the connections are re-established.

WEB RESEARCH SITES

All of the materials located on Gopherhosts can also be accessed through a Web browser, and the keyword searches described above can all be replicated on the Web. Additionally, the Web provides numerous keyword search engines of its own. Web search tools often allow not only a variety of different keyword searches but also some form of subject directory search. While some guides to the Internet make a sharp distinction between Web search tools which provide directories (or "trees") organized by subject and those which provide keyword searches, this is something of a false distinction. More common are the Web research tools which integrate both of these elements into a single, fluid interface.

The best way to begin a keyword search (indeed, any kind of search) on the Web is to find a "jump station," a Web page with links to various search tools, and, ideally, brief descriptions of each. If your institution does not support such a page, and you are not already familiar with one, we recommend you try the list at the University of Texas at Austin (*http://www.utexas.edu/search/*). Netscape's Net Search Directory is also an excellent location to begin a Web search. Connect to *http://home.netscape.com/escapes/search/* or, if you are using a Netscape Web browser, simply click on the "Net Search" button on the toolbar. In general, subject directories provide a good overview of the Internet material available on broadly-defined topics, and are therefore a good tool for the early stages of a research project. Keyword search engines enable much more comprehensive research on a topic, and are most useful when you have identified several keywords which will help you narrow the focus of your research. Browsing subject directories can help identify sub-categories of your broader topic, providing these additional keywords.

The Web searches described below represent only some of the innumerable research sites and search engines available on the Web (in contrast to Gopher, where only a handful exist). Whichever search you choose, the results will be returned to you as a list of hypertext links. Note that because some of the search engines scan the full text of files rather than just their titles, the items listed will not necessarily contain your keyword. You will sometimes need to follow even seemingly unrelated links to evaluate their usefulness. The list of search returns can be saved as a file and accessed during later sessions; however, to preserve the items as active links (and not just text), you must save the files in HTML format.

Alta Vista
http://altavista.digital.com/

A project sponsored by the Digital Equipment Corporation, Alta Vista provides a very fast search of either the Web or Usenet newsgroups. Alta Vista's real strength is its keyword search, which encompasses more than 30 million Web pages and several million newsgroup messages. Alta Vista will generally return more extensive results than other search tools, but more evaluation is required of the researcher to sift through this material to find the most relevant items. The advanced features of the Alta Vista search allow you to control both the selection criteria (Boolean terms, including NEAR), as well as "results ranking criteria" (matching documents are ranked according to a grade based on how many of the search terms each document contains, where the words are in the document, and how close to each other they are). While Alta Vista does not does not offer subject directories, it does offer a "random jumps" feature which is designed "to allow you to visit places in the Web you would never suspect existed." By choosing one of fifteen different general categories (e.g. Art, Interviews, Universities), a user is connected to a randomly-selected Web page. While the "random jumps" feature is a novel way of exploring the Web, it is not an especially useful tool for topic-driven academic research.

The Argus Clearinghouse
http://www.clearinghouse.net/

The Argus Clearinghouse is a central access point for guides which identify, describe, and evaluate Internet-based resources. Designed by librarians from the University of Michigan who share the belief that "intellectual labor is necessary to provide a qualitative assessment of the Internet's information," the Clearinghouse is primarily for specialized research at the university level. Guides on specific topics can be retrieved either with a keyword search, or by browsing through the subject categories, beginning with these primary categories: Arts & Humanities, Business and Employment, Communication, Computers and Information Technology, Education, Engineering, Environment, Government and Law, Health and Medicine, Places and Peoples, Recreation, Science and Mathematics, Social Sciences and Social Issues. An additional component of the Argus Clearinghouse is the "Internet Searching Center," which provides a simple index to the Internet tools and resources the Argus staff find to be the most useful.

All-in-One Search Page
http://www.albany.net/allinone/
The All-in-One Search Page, with more than 200 search tools in all, compiles search forms for all Web search engines. Search easily in categories such as: World Wide Web, General Interest, People, News, Publications, Desk Reference. (Note: the "categories" do not function like subject-directory trees for browsing, but are rather compilations of keyword search engines.) Once you perform a search, you will be connected to that particular search engine's home page for full use of its features; to return to the All-in-One Search Page, use the "back" arrow or the list of recent URLs on your Web browser's menu bar ("Go" on Netscape).

EINet Galaxy
http://www.einet.net/
The EINet Galaxy includes both a keyword search engine and subject directories. The keyword search supports Boolean operators and provides the option of searching the Galaxy pages (the subject trees and other pages on the Galaxy site), menu titles in Gopherspace, "hytelnet" (a hypertext database of Telnet sites), or the entire World Wide Web (complete text of documents, or the title or link texts only). The subject trees are intended for a professional audience in each category: Business and Commerce, Engineering and Technology, Government, Humanities, Law, Medicine, Reference, Science, Social Science. They provide general information that may interest the student researcher as well as announcements and other materials for professionals.

Excite
http://www.excite.com/
Excite Search offers a feature its creators proudly call searching the Web "by concept." That is, Excite's keyword feature not only searches for combinations of the search terms you enter, but also conceptually related terms. If, for example, you enter the term elderly people, Excite also searches automatically for documents containing the term senior citizen. Excite's coverage of the Web is estimated by the All-in-One Search Page as over one million Web pages. The scope of a keyword search can be set for the entire World Wide Web, an "Excite Web Guide" of 150,000 pages carefully selected "by Excite's experts," Usenet newsgroups, or "NewsTracker" (articles from over 300 Web-based publications). In addition to standard Boolean operators, Excite offers advanced search features that are explained at the site, such as a "more like this" link, radio buttons, and plus and minus signs. Excite's subject indexes organize by the following broad

categories: Arts and Entertainment, Business and Investing, Careers and Education, Computers and Internet, Games, Health and Science, Lifestyle, My Channel (a personalized information page with complex features), News, People and Chat, Politics, Shopping, Sports, Travel and Regional.

Infoseek
http://www.infoseek.com/
Infoseek is a good index of Web resources, for a general audience. Infoseek claims to have the world's largest directory of categorized Web pages (eclipsing Yahoo! in June, 1996). The directory is divided into these primary categories: Arts and Entertainment, Business, Computers, Education, Finance and Investment, Getting It Done (employment and finance issues), Health, Internet, Kids and Family Fun, Politics, Shopping, Sports, Travel and Leisure. Infoseek offers a "desk reference" section including Webster's dictionary, Roget's thesaurus and Bartlett's Quotations, as well as extensive directories of e-mail addresses, yellow pages, city maps, area codes, and zip codes.

Two keyword search tools make Infoseek distinct. Ultrasmart and Ultraseek. Ultraseek streamlines searches and is useful when you have a good idea of what you want to find. Ultrasmart enables users to narrow search results quickly by searching your previous results (unless you specify otherwise). A drop-down menu allows researchers to search other sets of information besides Web pages: Usenet newsgroups, news wire services, "premiere news" (from seven major national news organizations), e-mail addresses, company profiles, and Web FAQs. Many reviews of Infoseek praise the timeliness of its information, and its visually appealing interface.

Inter-Links
http://alabanza.com/kabacoff/Inter-Links/
The Inter-links home page offers a broad variety of features: links to all the major Internet search tools through the heading "Search the Net," links to online books and magazines and to "thousands of libraries," a Reference Shelf of dictionaries, encyclopedias and other sources of information, as well as categories for "News and Weather" and an extensive set of Internet and Web guides and tutorials. Inter-links also offers Web subject directories under the heading "topical resources," the primary divisions being: Diversity, Education, Employment, Fine Arts, Government, Health and Medicine, Law, Math and Science, Psychology.

The Internet Public Library
http://www.ipl.org/
The organization of this resource recalls that of a more traditional public library, with departments such as Reference, Teen, Youth, Magazines and

Serials, and Exhibits. Reference works and search tools include not only those categorized by the IPL, but some created by them as well (for example, a guide to the best search engines on the Web, with tips on how to use them effectively). Online serial publications can be searched by keyword or browsed by title, in alphabetical order or by subject. Permanent Exhibits in the IPL's "Exhibition Hall" include photographic essays and other works, on topics of American history and cultures. Hundreds of newspapers from dozens of countries are online and searchable at the IPL. Mimicking a reference desk where a researcher has the opportunity to ask questions of a librarian, the IPL offers interactive forms to allow you to send detailed questions to their reference staff.

The Internet Services List
http://www.spectracom.com/islist/
A resource with a simple hierarchy good for researchers new to the Web. The site offers a subject-directory listing of around eighty categories, from Agriculture to the World Wide Web. The Internet Services List does not itself offer a keyword search, but links to many search tools which do, either in local databases or "globally." The Internet Services List links to many Web sites, but also Gopher, Telnet and FTP resources that might not be uncovered by other search tools.

Library of Congress World Wide Web Home Page
http://lcWeb.loc.gov/
First and foremost, this site is an Internet showcase for the U.S. Library of Congress, and reflects all the resources of its analog in the physical world. The "American Memory" section presents extensive resources in American history. The THOMAS database provides full-text access to current bills under consideration in the U.S. Congress, and other Legislative resources; additional databases cover the other branches of the federal government, as well as state and local governments. Exhibitions in the Library of Congress are preserved in an online format on the site. Extensive Internet access is provided to the resources of the Library of Congress (e.g. the catalog, the research department). The entire Web site of the Library of Congress can be searched by keyword. The home page also organizes Internet resources into an extensive set of subject-categories, and links to multiple keyword search engines (for the Web as well as Gopher, FTP and Telnet sites).

Lycos
http://lycos.cs.cmu.edu/
The All-in-One page states that the "new" Lycos now indexes more than 90% of the Web. Reliable and fast, Lycos allows custom searching. It uses the matching parameters "loose," "fair" "good," "close," and "strong," but doesn't explain precisely how they narrow the search (although they clearly

do). Users can also specify how many of their terms the search engine should match at one time. Lycos indexes FTP and Gopher sites, but not Usenet newsgroups. Documents retrieved from a keyword search are ranked according to the number of search terms matched at once. The Lycos site touts the evaluative quality of much of its organization, presenting such resources as their "Top 5%" directory of best Web sites, and their choices of best online newspapers. Lycos offers subject-directory browsing for a general audience, with the primary categories being: News, Travel, Science, Culture, Business, fashion, Sports, Technology, Education, Shopping, Entertainment, Government, Money, Health, Lifestyle, Kids, Careers, Autos. Additional resources include news wire services, city guides, and searchable databases of people and companies.

Open Text Index
http://index.opentext.net/
The Open Text Index enables close control over search terms and the restriction of the search to Web document titles, summaries, URLs, first headings, or their entire texts. A very precise search can thus be made, but over a somewhat more limited scope (about two million Web pages). Usenet newsgroups, e-mail addresses, and "Current Events" (a dozen online newspapers) can also be searched.

Savvy Search
http://guaraldi.cs.colostate.edu:2000
Savvy Search, an experimental search system developed in the Computer Science Department of Colorado State University, enables searches with several engines simultaneously. It is thus a powerful technique both for enabling a more or less comprehensive search of everything available on the Web concerning a specific topic, as well as comparing the characteristics of different search engines. (Researchers can link directly from this site to each of the Web search tools which Savvy Search queries.) Search term options include "all query terms" (i.e. Boolean AND), "as a phrase" (a "literal search") and "any query terms" (Boolean OR). Display options include the ability to "Integrate Results," which combines duplicate search results and does not separate them by search engine (the process does add 45 seconds to the time of the search, however). Savvy Search also has international language capabilities.

WWW Virtual Library
http://www.w3.org/hypertext/DataSources/bySubject/Overview.html
A distributed subject catalog of Web resources. Primary divisions are into about 150 categories, including names of countries, areas of academic study (e.g. Asian Studies, Women's Studies), cultural forms (music, dance, theatre), scientific fields, and current issues (AIDS, environment). The

resources are cross-classified by type of service (i.e. Web, Gopher, FTP, Telnet). Annotated links to other Internet search tools are provided.

WebCrawler

http://Webcrawler.com/

WebCrawler was the first full-text search engine on the Internet (searching the full content of files, not just their titles). This powerful research tool began as a graduate student's research project at the University of Washington and was later sold to America Online and then to Excite, Inc. and became part of the Excite network of research tools. (Use of it remains free to the public.) WebCrawler's keyword search supports all the Boolean search operators (including NEAR and ADJ); if no operators are specified in a list of search terms, "OR" is the default (that is, WebCrawler will search for matches of any of the terms, in any combination). Results can be returned just as titles (for easier scanning), or with descriptions. A "relevance indicator" accompanies each term, scoring Web documents on the frequency and combination of search terms in them. WebCrawler provides an interactive map service for 22,000 U.S. cities. If your search terms include one of these cities (for example, "colleges in San Francisco"), the corresponding map is automatically offered among the search matches. WebCrawler also offers subject directories for browsing, with the following eighteen primary categories: Arts, Business, Chat, Computers, Education, Entertainment, Games, Health, Internet, Kids, Life, News, Recreation, Reference, Romance, Science, Sports, Travel.

Yahoo!

http://www.yahoo.com/

One of the first research tools to offer extensive directories of links organized by subject, Yahoo remains an extremely powerful resource. Designed primarily for a general and popular audience, Yahoo organizes material initially into fourteen broadly-defined categories: Arts and Humanities, Business and Economy, Computers and Internet, Education, Entertainment, Government, Health, News and Media, Recreation and Sports, Reference, Regional, Science, Social Science, and Society and Culture. From each of these categories, the researcher selects more narrowly-defined subjects.

While Yahoo has been noted primarily for the depth of its subject directories, it also offers a powerful keyword search. Initially, the researcher has the option to search Usenet newsgroups, a directory of e-mail addresses, or Yahoo categories themselves (a useful first step to browsing the directories that are related to your research topic. When searching Yahoo! make sure you carefully define the search area: "Yahoo categories" will search the names of directories themselves, while "Web Sites" will conduct a much broader search and retrieve specific Web pages related to your topic. Boolean search strings are supported; additionally, if you are looking only for very current material, you have the option to limit the search to listings added within a specified period of time from one day to three years.

SAVING THE PRODUCT

In addition to familiarizing yourself with the methods of organization on the Internet, and learning about keyword searches and Boolean strings, there are strategies for Internet browsing which can help make your work more productive.

The first and most basic principle you need to remember is that, especially with client software, whatever you are looking at can be easily downloaded and saved. With text files this is often as simple as choosing the "Save as..." command, which will save the material either onto the computer's hard drive or a diskette. Depending on the browser you use, you may also have the option of saving graphic files, sound files, and other media. Sometimes, the designer of a Gopherhost or a Web site will have programmed another method for downloading files—for example, clicking on the links of a Web page might download the item to your computer. Look for FAQ and "readme" files located on the specific sites for further information.

Downloading text files is especially useful if there is a limit to the number of Internet-connected computers at your institution. You can take these files and read them on any computer, freeing up the Internet-connected computer for research by other students.

Although the tremendous amount of material available on the Internet can be seductive, downloading everything about a particular topic may not be a practical search strategy. You need to choose selectively in order for your research to be effective. In general, skim a few online sources to get a sense of the broad context of your chosen research topic. Note those sources that you think will be most useful, and as you focus and narrow your topic, read these sources more carefully and follow links within them to new research materials. Remember, you can quickly evaluate a source's usefulness for your topic by performing keyword searches within the text of the document looking for occurrences of terms that you know are important to your particular topic.

The format of materials you encounter can also be important. Text files, for example, will usually be sufficient for the "traditional" research paper. Since graphics, sound or video files, take more time to download and save than text files, you may be better off accessing them after you have gathered and examined an adequate number of text files. If, on the other hand you are building multimedia projects, you may need to examine these files sooner. If you cannot decide whether you will need a file of any sort later, it is safest, because of the changing nature of the Internet, to save a copy, as well as note the address of the site from which it came.

Finally, you should make use of *bookmarks* and *hotlists*. These features save the URL for the pages you access with your browser, adding them to a list of other sites. Clicking an item on the list allows you to connect directly to that particular document. Since every file on the Web receives its own URL, the items on your hotlist may be general sites (for example, the opening window or home page of an institution) or specific documents or even pages with interesting designs that you would like to imitate. All can be useful.

CHAPTER 6

Node Construction Ahead: The Web and Hypertext Markup Language

WHAT IS HTML?

In this chapter, we discuss the fundamentals of building of Web pages using *Hypertext Markup Language (HTML)*. HTML is the scripting language which is used to turn plain text and other elements (such as images) into the integrated pages we see on the Web. As we stated in the previous chapter, the Web represents a convergence of hypertext, multimedia, and Internet connectivity (subsuming in the process many of the functions of earlier Internet media). HTML gives the Web its exciting power to present ideas and in a sense is behind its exponential growth. Over the long term, building Web pages in HTML contributes to the research process, as students enter into ongoing conversations by posting their ideas onto the Internet and receiving feedback on them.

Some elements of the spatial makeup of the Web were discussed in the previous chapter: that every Web page has its own particular address (called a URL), that pages are grouped together in sites produced by a single user or organization, that these groups of pages reside on Web servers, and that the movement from page to page is a fluid one. (If you are unfamiliar with the Web, particularly Web servers and browsers, you may want to review Chapter 5.) In this chapter, you will learn how to produce Web pages and upload them to a server so that they can be viewed by the Internet-connected world. The process of HTML scripting is surprisingly easy and can be learned in multiple stages. Anyone can produce interesting, attractive documents with only the most fundamental commands and with increasing knowledge add more sophisticated elements.

One of the first concepts that Web builders should understand is the basic relationship between a Web page and its underlying HTML script. Say you were looking with a Web browser at this section of a page:

This will be normal text

This will be bold

Looking at the same example with a text editor would reveal the HTML script:

This will be normal text
<HR>
<B>This will be bold</B>
In HTML, a pair of bracketed commands like <B> . . . </B> instruct the browser to format the text between the commands. Additional commands like <HR> ("horizontal rule") affect the layout of the page.

HTML WRITERS AND HELPER APPLICATIONS

Working with Web pages, more than any other Internet activity discussed in this book, requires a variety of programs. Check with your systems administrator about which programs your institution supports. In addition to a browser for viewing and navigating the Web, you will need:

- A text editor or word processor to compose your HTML files. While you can compose HTML with any word processor, we recommend using an HTML editor which will automate many of the scripting commands and offer other useful features.
- An FTP client to upload your files to a Web server so that browsers can access them. (See Chapter 1 for information on FTP.)
- Helper applications to open graphic, sound and video files as well as to handle more advanced browser functions. These applications can vary greatly and should be coordinated with your Web browser and your workstation's capacity.

WORKING WITH NEW MATERIALS

Successful Web building first requires some knowledge of the organizational structures of Web projects and an understanding of the relationship between Web pages as viewed through a browser and the underlying HTML documents that produce them. Before you begin to build, browse the Web looking for sites with interesting hypertextual designs. Notice how these designs are different from the papers you have written. Traditional papers can be posted on the Web by adding the necessary HTML formatting commands, but the Web audience is likely to skip long pages of scrollable text in favor of sites that incorporate graphics and offer more opportunity for the reader to interact. Some critics take this as a sign that the medium presents information superficially, but an emphasis on bells and whistles, on delivering information with the help of new media like the Web and in non-linear ways, should not preclude critical thinking.

VIEWING THE SOURCE

The HTML viewing functions of most browsers displays the underlying HTML document that organizes a Web page (in most browsers this is a menu command, such as View Source). Initiating this function downloads a copy of the HTML file and opens it in a text editor showing the text along with the different HTML commands that were used to make the page.

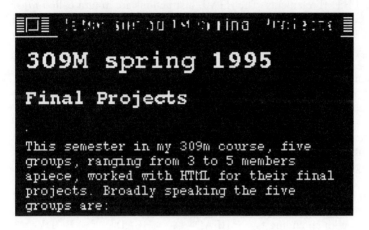

Viewing the source for the above page would reveal the HTML commands that control the format of the document:

<TITLE>309M spring 1995 Final Projects</TITLE>
<H1>309M spring 1995</H1>
<H2>Final Projects</H2>
<HR>This semester in my 309m course, five groups, ranging from 3 to 5 members apiece, worked with HTML for their final projects. Broadly speaking the five groups are:

Web building takes place in this underlying HTML document. Note how theabove sample from the browser has the title in the window bar at the top of the page "309M spring 1995 Final Projects." Looking at the source document reveals the command that places that information in the window bar:

<TITLE>309M spring 1995 Final Projects</TITLE>.

The same holds true for the headings, the larger text that begins the document proper:

<H1>309M spring 1995 </H1>
<H2>Final Projects</H2>
<HR> This semester in my 309m course, five groups...

The largest heading in the sample "309M spring 1995" is controlled by the <H1> . . . </H1> command. HTML offers six heading levels, with <H1> being the largest and <H6> the smallest. Between the headings and the body text, a line is drawn across the top of the browser page by using the horizontal rule command <HR>.

55

HTML instructions, together with the text to which the instructions apply, are called HTML elements. The HTML instructions are in turn called *tags*, and are comprised of the element name surrounded by left and right angle brackets. For example, all Web pages begin with the element <HTML> so that Web browsers immediately identify the document as an HTML file.

Most elements mark blocks of the document text for purposes of formatting. The end of a formatted section is marked by an ending tag, with the leading slash character "/" in front of the element name: </HTML>.

Some elements are "empty"—that is, they do not affect a block of the document. These elements do not require an ending tag. For example, the single tag <BR> breaks a line of text, continuing on the next line.

HTML documents themselves are broken into two main sections, the head and the body. Each section begins with a tag designating the section, and closes with an ending tag: <HEAD> . . . </HEAD>   <BODY> . . </BODY>

The head portion specifies information that browsers and servers use to search and organize documents. The most important component of a document's head is the title element, which provides the information that appears at the top of the browsing window and is used for most keyword searches: <TITLE> . . . </TITLE>

Often, JavaScripts are also placed in the document head, to manage information and perform complex functions (a message forum, for example). The majority of additional commands, however, will be incorporated into the body of the document.

IMAGES AND LINKS

Inline images and links are two slightly more complex HTML commands, used extensively in Web page design. An image which has been inserted into the design of a Web page is called an inline image.

SAMPLE OF AN INLINE IMAGE AND A TEXTUAL LINK

Air Pollution: Air pollution, **including ozone pollution** is becoming one of the most damaging problems in the world today.

In this sample the phrase "including ozone pollution" appearing in boldface (in colored text in most browsers) is linked or hot text. As discussed in Chapter 5, a link is a hypertextual function that connects documents, sites, and other media. (Note that "link" is commonly used both as a noun to indicate the actual connection between one node and another, and as a verb to indicate the process by which this connection is achieved.)

Viewing the source of the sample above would reveal
<IMG ALIGN=bottom SRC="clouds.gif"> Air Pollution: Air pollution, <A HREF="*http://www.greenpeace.org/~ozone/*"> including ozone pollution</A> is becoming one of the most damaging problems in the world today.

The first element in this sample, the inline image, works like a formatting command by using a single set of brackets (<IMG ALIGN=bottom SRC="clouds.gif">). Within those brackets, additional information is provided. The inline image cue (IMG) is followed by information specifying the layout of any subsequent text in relationship to the image (ALIGN=bottom). Within the command there is also information about the name or source of the image (SRC="clouds.gif"). The SRC= element tells the browser where to find the image and can include an entire URL if the image does not reside in the same file system as the HTML document. In this case, the browser is told to find the image "clouds.gif" (which is in the same directory in the local file system), to place the image in the Web page and to align any text which comes after it at the bottom of the image.

A SAMPLE URL

Recall that every file on the Web has a unique address or URL. The sample above demonstrates both a local and a remote URL. The source for the inline image (SRC="clouds.gif") is a local file. Thus, the file name, "clouds.gif," serves as the local URL.

The sample address following the <A HREF> element utilizes a remote URL (*http://www.greenpeace.org/~ozone/*). Unlike the local URL, the entire address must be given, since this file is located on a different Web server.

The sample also illustrates the basics of the HTML link command. In this case, the element provides additional information but works with paired brackets to designate the hot text, or anchor, for the link:
<A HREF= "*http://www.greenpeace.org/~ozone/*"> including ozone pollution</A>
The information that is given in the opening tag indicates that an anchor for a link is being established and gives a reference which tells the browser what to do when someone clicks on the hot text. In this case, the browser is told to go to a page sponsored by Greenpeace with information about

ozone and the environment. The entire URL is specified, which will send the reader to the page: *http://www.greenpeace.org/~ozone/*. All of this information is contained within the first set of brackets that makes up the command. The tag </A> merely works to close the link element. As with the <TITLE> . . . </TITLE> element, everything in between the two sets of brackets will be acted upon by the command. In this case, the phrase "including ozone pollution" will become hot text when viewed by a browser, and clicking on the phrase will activate the link to Greenpeace.

These commands are given merely to illustrate the basic functionality of HTML. This section is not intended as a complete list of all HTML possibilities. The HTML Documentation Site (*http://www.utoronto.ca/ Webdocs/HTMLdocs/NewHTML/htmlindex.htm*) and at the Yahoo HTML site (*http://www.yahoo.com/Computers/World_Wide_Web/ HTML/*). There are also many HTML editors available by FTP as freeware which automate the process of composing in HTML. These editors are not necessary, but can be especially useful when dealing with more complex commands. Whether you use an HTML editor or not, however, your students should understand the basic structure of these commands so they can check the HTML information when a link or image is not working, or when a page needs modification.

BUILDING LOCALLY

The process of revising Web pages may feel unfamiliar because of the need to move back and forth continually between the HTML document and the browser in order to see how a page is displayed. After making changes to a an HTML file the author reloads the revised document in the browser. This is why Web authors most frequently build their files within single folders or directories on a diskette or local hard drive, rather than on the Web server where the file will eventually reside.

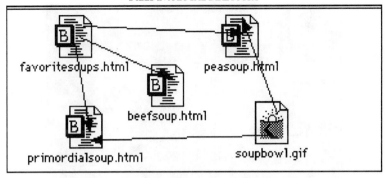

The sample above shows several different files which all exist within a single directory, or folder. Note that the project makes use of both HTML files and graphics files, as designated by the suffixes .html and .gif on their file names, respectively. On the Web, the major types of files are HTML documents (.html), text files (.txt), graphics files (.gif) and (.jpeg), movie files (.mpeg) and (.mov), and sound files (.wav) and (.au). In order for browsers to read the files they must be named with the proper suffixes. File names in a PC format will use the shortened three character suffixes: .htm, .jpg and .mpg. Note also that this sample uses all lower-case characters with no spaces between them in its file names. This strategy is important because some servers handle spaces and upper-case file names differently. While some browsers and situations are more forgiving, Web links are case-sensitive. Many Web authors follow the convention of using only lower-case characters with no spaces between them in both file names and their HTML links. This saves time uncovering typographical mistakes that cause broken links.

Logistically, local files simplify Web building and revision a great deal. Making links, for example, is much simpler if you can enter the relatively brief name of a local file instead of a lengthy URL. Building locally will also make things easier when moving files to your Web server; if all of the links work within a directory on a local level, then the links should continue to work regardless of their final position on a server.

WORKING WITH SUB-DIRECTORIES WHEN BUILDING LOCALLY

The graphic below illustrates the paths necessary to work with sub-directories when building Web pages. It is only necessary to specify file and directory names when working on a local disk or drive to build Web pages.

However, if students wish to link to materials within a sub-directory or folder, they can specify the sub-directory, followed by a slash "/" and the file name.

In the example above, the path "gills/halibut.html" links to a file called "halibut" which resides within a folder called "gills." To move back up in the directory structure, a link can use the "../" command in a URL along with the path to the document or file to which you wish to connect. For example, to make a link from the file called "halibut.html" in the sample to the file "fish.html" in the directory directly above it in the hierarchy, a user would enter the URL "../fish.html." You can use a series of "/" and "../" commands to navigate through multiple directory levels. As with all links, students should name their files without spaces, and using lower-case characters.

SERVING IT UP

Serving files involves two major activities: 1) overseeing the behind-the-scenes operations of the Web server, including setting up form and imagemap routines, and running software which provides the proper protocol for sharing files on the Web, and 2) managing directory structures and files which reside on the Web server. Organizing your files and uploading them to a server may require some extra time and energy, especially if you are uncomfortable with the various technologies. Whatever your level of technological knowledge, we recommend that you coordinate with your Web administrators as you work through the various tasks involved in serving your files.

Usually your computation center or some other institutional entity will be responsible for the behind-the-scenes operations of the Web server, so you will probably not be involved in the first of these two activities (if you do need information about the server-side operations of the Web, see *http://Web66.coled.umn.edu/ Cookbook/*). Some institutions will provide students with individual accounts for Web building, but in many cases, the instructor will be responsible for managing files for the entire class.

Before considering the ways that you might upload finished files to the server, you should think about the directory structures that will house those files. If you are familiar with directories in DOS or a folder filing system in either Windows or Macintosh, then the organization of Web files will be fairly comfortable. Rather than uploading all your files into a single directory, we suggest that you first organize your server space by making subdirectories. If you are creating two or more Web sites, for example, you might provide a directory for each of them and, within those directories, you might make additional subdirectories. The organization will depend on your own needs, but considering these structures early in the building process will save you considerable time and effort in the long run.

Finally, you will need to upload the finished files to the server, most likely using an FTP client (see Chapter 1). If you have built local files (see "Building Locally" above), you may be able to load all of your directories at once, depending upon your FTP client. Otherwise, you will need to place files on the sever individually. In any case, check that the final organization of the directories and files that you load to the server mirrors the structure of any projects developed locally. Additionally, when loading files, make sure that HTML documents and any text files are sent as "ASCII text" or "text only" and that other media are transported as "binary" or "raw data." Make sure that file names remain unaltered during the uploading process. Finally, after you have placed files on the server, you should check the links with a browser to ensure that nothing has gone wrong.

WEAVING A WEB COMPOSITION

Despite the strange appearance of some of the link and image commands above, most people find HTML scripting rather simple. There are a finite number of commands, and once you are comfortable with the process of building HTML documents with a text editor and viewing them with a browser, the composition itself goes quite smoothly. More important for the success of your Web document may be the ways that the organization of the project works to further your rhetorical goals.

Because of the hypertextual nature of the Web, the major themes of a document or the strands of an argument can be organized as several different nodes of a project. A *node* is a hypertextual site which organizes multiple links. Nodes can contain any combination of text, links, graphics, sound, and video. When planning documents, consider the potential paths that a reader might take to reach these nodes. Often an initial *index page* provides the organizational structure that maps the site—often the "starting point" for a hypertext. The index page (usually named "index.html") is in some ways analogous to the topic paragraph of a traditional essay. This page can be used to map out the direction of the project and to give the reader enough information to make informed choices about the possibilities for reading the document. Since Web projects can sometimes turn into long lists of unexplained links, instructors may want to have students map out their ideas on paper before composing their initial page.

Since the initial page of a Web site determines to a great extent the paths that a reader might take through a document, this page should be organized so that it works to achieve your purpose. For example, you might develop in detail one of the major claims of an argument by using a sub-node that must be accessed by following a link from the initial page; that link should appear in a way that signals readers to follow it if they are having questions about that claim.

Never develop nodes under the assumption that a reader has understood information from (or even visited) a previous node. If an idea is crucial to the argument, develop it either initially or with repetition at the various sub-nodes that rely on the idea. Indicate in some way how each node relates to the other nodes of the site.

IMAGEMAPS AND GRAPHICAL LINKS

One way to maximize the organizational potential of a Web site is to incorporate the use of imagemaps into their layout. An imagemap is a graphic image that has been "mapped" by HTML commands so that clicking on different portions of it will link the user to different sites or files, most often to different areas of a Web site. The author configures hot spots on the image and a reader who clicks on one of the hot spots will be sent to whatever link has been assigned to that spot.

SAMPLE IMAGEMAP

The sample above uses a composite image to link to the major nodes of a project. These maps can be useful as they provide a visual navigational tool for the site. We should caution that not all servers support imagemaps, and configuring the hot spots and links is somewhat sophisticated. Check with your server administrator before deciding to use imagemaps (for more information about making imagemaps, see (*http://www.utoronto.ca/ Webdocs/HTMLdocs/NewHTML /serv-ismap.html*).

You do not need to use an image map to add graphical links to your Web site. By placing an image in a Web page (see below) and then creating a link from that image, a student can design a site that uses visual elements to facilitate a reader's movement without having to learn the complex operation of imagemaps. We recommend that small images be used to make links and that the student consider images that convey a sense of the link to be followed; a small picture of a house, for example, could be used to indicate a return link to the *home page*. (Remember that home page is the conventional name given to a central site on the World Wide Web. This name can be used both for the central page of a university or business site and for the personal page of an individual.)

WORKING WITH GRAPHICS

Depending on your facilities, you will likely have several options when it comes to using graphics on the Web. If you have graphics programs you can create your own images or manipulate existing images for use on the Web. If not, then you can use some of the many images that have been made available at various archival sites around the Web. If you have storage space considerations, you can also use the URL of an image that exists somewhere else on the Web in your own documents. Linking to an image on another site will display that image in your own Web page. Most Web sites are fairly liberal about the use of their images, but you should investigate site policies and respect the considerations of intellectual property when linking to or downloading images from around the Web (see the Appendix for more information on copyright considerations). A good policy is to ask permission with an e-mail message whenever you duplicate an image or link to a site.

Once you have appropriate graphics, you should consider the most effective way of incorporating them into your pages. First, the relatively large size of some images can make viewing Web pages frustrating, especially if a reader is using a modem to access your site. We recommend that inline images be less than thirty kilobytes (30k); you should link to larger images as separate files, providing descriptions and a clear indication of their sizes. You may also want to supply a reduced version of the image, so that readers can glance at larger graphics without taking the time to download each one. Overloading a page, even with small images, can make viewing difficult as browsers must continually return to the server to load image after image. Additionally, some users do not have inline image functions and others disable the function on their browsers, so students should use the "ALT" attribute in their image commands (for example, <IMG ALIGN=bottom SRC="clouds.gif" ALT = "a picture of clouds">). The "ALT" option will display a textual alternative if a browser is unable to load an image.

Along with the logistical considerations involved in using graphics on the Web, you should consider the aesthetic impact of images in your compositions. One helpful suggestion is to think of the "screen full" as the rhetorical unit of Web compositions. If you place an eight by ten inch graphic at the top of a Web page you will have little room for anything else. While some situations may call for an entirely graphical page, we think that a mixture of text and graphics makes best use of the Web's multimedia potential. A very large graphic leaves no room for text to converse with the image, to contextualize it, or to introduce the page.

Be aware also of a tendency for images to produce a false sense of explication. If images make an integral part of your document (for example, using movie stills to evaluate aspects of a film), then textual explications should accompany graphics and make clear connections between the images and the larger themes of the project. Most important to remember is that the images should not be used unnecessarily; they should strive to fulfill the rhetorical aims of the project. At the same time,keep in mind that the Web is a graphical environment. The audience for Web pages often expects something more than plain text, and students establish credible Web ethos by incorporating images into their pages, even if those images are only the various balls, colored lines, and other icons commonly found throughout the Web.

USING FORMS TO INTERACT WITH A WEB AUDIENCE

A *form* is a mechanism by which Web browsers allow users to send information back to the server. If at all possible, we recommend that you include a comment form with each of your Web projects. Most comment forms are configured to send e-mail to the author of a Web page.

SAMPLE COMMENT FORM

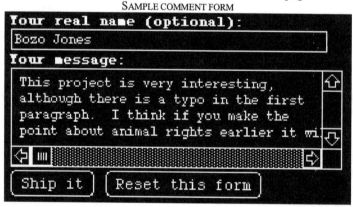

By using interactive comment forms, you can engage the Web's global audience. As with imagemaps, the ability to use interactive forms will depend upon the capacities of your Web server. Check with your server administrator about using forms. Many browsers now support the <MAILTO> HTML command, which can be configured to send e-mail to an author. If your server does not support forms, you should consider including a <MAILTO> option in your pages to facilitate contact. While the sample above shows the most basic contact form, you can modify forms to include fields for other information. (For more on forms, see

64

http://www.yahoo.com/Computers/World_Wide_WeProgramming/Forms/). The feedback gathered through forms can be highly rewarding. To maximize this potential, submit your URL to some of the large database sites around the Web, circulate your URL on relevant listservs and newsgroups, and announce it to various site administrators so that they can provide links to your pages. The sprawling nature of the Web makes publicizing your pages a task that goes hand in hand with carefully constructing them.

STYLE CONVENTIONS ON THE WEB

Although the Web is a medium that for the most part remains uncharted, some stylistic axioms are already beginning to be formulated.

Use graphics modestly. Multimedia, especially graphics, are easily incorporated into Web pages, and the initial temptation is to overload a page with pictures, employing the graphical capabilities of HTML simply because they are new and exciting. You should note, however, the rhetorical connections between the text and media on a page. Like a successfully integrated quotation, effective images are contextualized and related to relevant points of a document. Images should add another level of understanding to a work rather than confuse or distract a reader. Not only do large, irrelevant graphic files show bad style and overwhelm a reader, but they also can bog down a computer system. Some observers also feel that graphics should not be any wider than the standard size of a browsing window (about 6.75 inches).

Insert navigational links that help the reader. The author should provide the reader with links to previous pages and to other relevant sections of the project. Usually, navigational links are at the bottom of the page, though the document itself may dictate their placement.

Sign and date your Web pages. Again, most authors put this information at the bottom of the page. Many incorporate a contact function into their signatures by either providing a link to a comment form or by using the <MAILTO> command. Because readers will sometimes return to a site periodically to see if any new materials have been added, the page also should include the date of the last revision of the site.

Use language in links that tells what they lead to. Remember that a link could lead to a Web site anywhere in the world. Whether you are linking to another section of you own document or to a remote site, you should explain why you are providing the link and what the reader can expect to find by following the links. For example, the conventional hot text phrase "click here" fails to convey any information about the link. A better phrase will succinctly and clearly describe the link to the reader.

While these general recommendations are important, we'd like to suggest that HTML style is not yet a well-defined, homogenous set of conventions. As the Web evolves, it will likely be put to a variety of new rhetorical purposes, and each of these will present its own demands and stylistic choices.

A GUIDE TO HTML COMMANDS

Headings

```
<H1> . . . </H1>—largest header
<H2> . . . </H2>
<H3> . . . </H2>
<H4> . . . </H4>
<H5> . . . </H5>
<H6> . . . </H6>—smallest header
```

The placement of the headings may also be dictated by adding to the heading element an ALIGN attribute, now supported by most Web browsers. The possible values for headings are ALIGN="left," ALIGN="center," or ALIGN="right." For example, the element
```
<H1 ALIGN="center"> . . . </H1>
```
will both give the text between the tags the largest heading size, and center that text on the page. Note the use of quotes within the tag itself. If no ALIGN attribute is included, the heading will default to left-side alignment.

Font Styles

`<B> . . . </B>`	**Bold-face text**
`<I> . . . </I>`	*Italicized text*
`<U> . . . </U>`	<u>Underlined text</u>
`<TT> . . . </TT>`	Typewriter font
`<STRIKE> . . . </STRIKE>`	~~Strike-through text~~
`<SUP> . . . </SUP>`	Superscript text
`<SUB> . . . </SUB>`	Subscript text
`<BIG> . . . </BIG>`	Large font
`<SMALL> . . . </SMALL>`	Small font
`<CENTER> . . . </CENTER>`	Centered material

Lists & Menus

Definition list—presents a list of items with definitions for each appearing on an indented line below.

```
<DL>
<DT> First term
<DD> Definition
<DT> Next term
<DD> Definition
</DL>
```

Unnumbered list—presents a list with bullets appearing before each item	`<UL>`
	`<LI>` First item in the list
	`<LI>` Next item in the list
	`</UL>`

Numbered list—presents a list with numbers appearing before each item.	`<OL>`
	`<LI>` First item in the list
	`<LI>` Next item in the list
	`</OL>`

Menu—presents a list in which each item appears indented.	`<MENU>`
	`<LI>` First item in the menu
	`<LI>` Next item
	`</MENU>`

Links

The most common is the link to a document or file:

<A HREF="URL/file name"> . . . </A>

You can also make a link to a target within a document. Begin by placing a target anchor in the desired spot in the document.

<A NAME="target name">

Next make a link to the target by using the "#" sign and specifying the target name in the link information

<A HREF="#target name"> . . . </a>

You can also link to a sound, graphic, or video file by specifying the proper file name in the link information

`<A HREF="URL/filename.gif">...</A>`	links to a gif image.
`<A HREF="URL/filename.jpg">...</A>`	links to a jpeg image
`<A HREF="URL/filename.mpg">...</A>`	links to an mpeg movie
`<A HREF="URL/filename.mov">...</A>`	links to a Quicktime movie
`<A HREF="URL/filename.au">...</A>`	links to a sound file
`<A HREF ="URL/filename.wav">...</A>`	links to a sound file

Inline Images

Inline images are graphics which are incorporated into the layout of a Web page. To place an inline image in a document select the point in the document where the image should appear and use the command

<IMG ALIGN=bottom SRC="imagefilename.gif">

The align element of the command ("bottom" in the example) controls where surrounding text will appear in relation to the graphic. The standard alignments are "top," "middle" and "bottom," although many browsers support "left" and "right" as well. With "left" and "right" alignment, the image is aligned with the selected margin, and the text following the image element in the HTML script flows around the image.

With any inline image, remember to include an ALT attribute in the element, which specifies an alternative textual description of the image (add

ALT=". . ." to the string of attributes in the <IMG> tag). This feature is a courtesy to users with slower connections who have "turned off" automatic image loading on their Web browsers.

Background Feature
The background attribute allows the user to specify an image file to use as a background for the Web page. This attribute is applied to the body element, discussed above. For example, at the beginning of the body section of a Web page, the element

    <BODY BACKGROUND="imagename.gif">

tiles the window background with the designated GIF image. When the background attribute is utilized, the end tag to the body section is still simply: </BODY>.

Colors
Recently, the use of color on Web pages has expanded widely, and is supported by most Web browsers. Colors can be given to a number of page elements. In HTML, colors are designated by six-character codes representing their relative red/green/blue (RGB) values. Because of the incredible complexity of these codes, we recommend you use an HTML editor which supports the application of color. In such an editor, a shade is selected from a color wheel and the corresponding RGB values are placed automatically in the HTML script. Also, you might refer to one of the many Web sites that provides the codes for the 256 most commonly-used shades (for example, *http://www.onr.com/user/lights/netcol.html*).

Colors are usually applied as attributes to the <BODY> element, and should be specified in the opening tag. If one of the following attributes is used, they should all be specified in order to avoid color conflicts. If, for example, a visitor to your page has set the Web browser to display text in the same color you gave to your background, this would make the page unreadable.

<BODY BGCOLOR="#rrggbb">	sets the background color for the page as a whole
<BODY TEXT="#rrggbb">	sets the text color for the page as a whole
<BODY LINK="#rrggbb">	sets the unvisited link color for the page as a whole
<BODY VLINK="#rrggbb">	sets the visited link color for the page as a whole
<BODY ALINK="#rrggbb">	sets the activated link color for the page as a whole

All these attributes should be specified in a single <body> tag, like so:
    <BODY BGCOLOR="#rrggbb" TEXT="#rrggbb"
    LINK="#rrggbb" VLINK="#rrggbb" ALINK="#rrggbb">

Colors may also be applied to selected text within the body of a Web page. The element

<FONT COLOR="#rrggbb"> . . . </FONT>

will set the color of the text between the tags to the designated shade.

Tables

HTML tables are contained within <TABLE> . . . </TABLE> tags. The fundamental elements of an HTML table are <CAPTION>, which defines a caption for the table, and <TR>, which defines a table row. Each row in turn contains cells, either for a header, defined by <TH>, or for data, defined by <TD>. (Although in this example we are using only numerical data, text and even graphic files can be entered in a data cell as well.) Each cell should be closed with the appropriate ending tag, either </TH> or </TD>.

The caption may be aligned to the top, bottom, left, or right of the table by adding an ALIGN attribute to the <CAPTION> tag. By default. a table is flush with the left margin, but it can be centered by placing the entire table script within <CENTER> . . . </CENTER> tags. Additionally, a BORDER attribute may be added to the <TABLE> tag, which indicates that the table should be drawn with a border around it and between each of the table's cells. Adding a value (in number of pixels) sets the outer border of the table to the specified width.

To combine all these features, then, the following script:

```
<TABLE BORDER>
<CAPTION ALIGN="bottom">This is the Table Caption</CAPTION>
<TR> <TH>Heading 1</TH> <TH>Heading 2</TH> <TH>Heading 3</TH> </TR>
<TR> <TD>0.8</TD> <TD>1.2</TD> <TD>4.6</TD> </TR>
<TR> <TD>5.4</TD> <TD>0.44</TD> <TD>3.7</TD> </TR>
<TR> <TD>2.5</TD> <TD>6.2</TD> <TD>3.5</TD> </TR>
</TABLE>
```

produces a table displayed as:

Heading 1	Heading 2	Heading 3
0.8	1.2	4.6
5.4	0.44	3.7
2.5	6.2	3.5

This is the Table Caption

You can also experiment with adding the CELLPADDING= and CELLSPACING= attributes to the <TABLE> element, which dictate (in number of pixels) the amount of space surrounding the contents of cells, and the width of the borders between cells, respectively. More complex tables are clearly illustrated on the Netscape Web site, at *http://home.netscape.com/assist/net_sites/tables.html.* With their more advanced features, HTML tables can provide not simply a way to present data clearly, but a strategy for Web page design itself. Examine the text Connections by Anderson, Benjamin, and Paredes-Holt for discussion of this strategy.

CHAPTER 7

Documenting Electronic Sources

Major documentation systems like the APA and the MLA have recently incorporated guidelines for citing Internet sources in their style guides; however, we think their suggestions fail to provide the necessary citation information for Internet resources because they duplicate the format of traditional documentation forms without accommodating the particular demands of the Internet.

The MLA Handbook offers the following guide for Internet sources.

Material accessed through a computer network

1. Name of author (if given)
2. Title of article or document (in quotation marks)
3. Title of the journal, newsletter or conference (underlined)
4. Volume number, issue number or other identifying number
5. Year of date of publication (in parenthesis)
6. Number of pages or paragraphs (if given) or n.pag ("no pagination")
7. Publication medium (on-line)
8. Name of computer network
9. Date of access

A sample entry would look like this:

Moulthrop, Stuart. "You Say You Want a Revolution? Hypertext and the Laws of Media." <u>Postmodern Culture</u> 1. (1991): 53 pars. On-line BITNET. 10 Jan. 1993

According to the MLA, at the end of the entry you may add as supplementary information the electronic address you used to access the document; precede the address with the word "Available." They note that "[y]our instructor may require this information."

Though it is a convention that tries to indicate the existence of Internet sources, this system does little to handle the unique nature of Internet publications. Simply telling a reader that a source can be found "on-line" does little to help a researcher find the source document. It would be very difficult to locate this source again and to determine if you had the same version of the document. Because of the Internet's vast scope and changing nature, it is especially important to provide the exact path by which you found a document and to distinguish between the date you found the source and it's publication date (if it has one).

ACW DOCUMENTATION

Janice R. Walker of the Department of English at the University of South Florida has developed a style guide for handling Internet resources that distinguishes between different protocols and highlights the importance of addresses in each. The components of her reference citation are simply:

Author's Last Name, First Name. "Title of Work." *Title of Complete Work.* [protocol and address] [path] (date of message or visit).

In addition, Walker has placed a style sheet on the World Wide Web that provides a documentation system for all the Internet media we cover in this book. A copy of this style sheet follows. We would recommend providing this style sheet for your students as an addition to the MLA handbook in order to cite Internet sources.

INTERNET STYLE SHEET

also available at
http://www.cas.usf.edu/english/walker/mla.html
(Endorsed by the Alliance for Computers & Writing)

FTP (File Transfer Protocol) Sites
To cite files available for downloading via FTP, give the author's name (if known), the full title of the paper in quotation marks, and the address of the FTP site along with the full path to follow to find the paper, and the date of access.

Bruckman, Amy. "Approaches to Managing Deviant Behavior in Virtual Communities." ftp.media.mit.edu pub/asb/papers/deviance-chi94 (4 Dec.1994).

WWW Sites (World Wide Web)
(Available via Lynx, Netscape, Other Web Browsers)
To cite files available for viewing/downloading via the World Wide Web, give the author's name (if known), the full title of the work in quotation marks, the title of the complete work if applicable in italics, the full http address, and the date of visit.

Burka, Lauren P. "A Hypertext History of Multi-User Dimensions." *MUD History.* http://www.ccs.neu.edu/home/lpb/mud-history.html (5 Dec. 1994).

Telnet Sites
(Sites and Files available via the Telnet protocol)
List the author's name (if known), the title of the work (if shown)   in quotation marks, the title of the full work if applicable in italics, and the complete Telnet address, along with directions to access the publication, along with the date of visit.

Gomes, Lee. "Xerox's On-Line Neighborhood: A Great Place to Visit." *Mercury News* 3 May 1992. Telnet lambda.parc.xerox.com 8888, @go #50827, press 13 (5 Dec. 1994).

Synchronous Communications
(MOOs, MUDs, IRC, etc.)
Give the name of the speaker(s) and type of communication (i.e., Personal Interview), the address if applicable and the date in parentheses.

Pine_Guest. Personal Interview. Telnet world.sensemedia.net 1234 (12 Dec.1994).

WorldMOO Christmas Party. Telnet world.sensemedia.net 1234 (24 Dec. 1994).

GOPHER Sites
(Information available via Gopher search protocols)
For information found using Gopher search protocols, list the author's name, the title of the paper in quotation marks, any print publication information, and the Gopher search path followed to access the information, including the date that the file was accessed.

Quittner, Joshua. "Far Out: Welcome to Their World Built of MUD." Published in *Newsday*, 7 Nov. 1993. Gopher /University of Koeln/About MUDs, MOOs and MUSEs in Education/Selected Papers/newsday (5 Dec. 1994).

E-mail, Listserv, and Newslist Citations

Give the author's name (if known), the subject line from the posting   in quotation marks, and the address of the listserv or newslist, along with the date. For personal e-mail listings, the address may be omitted.

Bruckman, Amy S. "MOOSE Crossing Proposal."
    mediamoo@media.mit.edu (20 Dec. 1994).

Seabrook, Richard H. C. "Community and Progress."
    cybermind@jefferson.village.virginia.edu (22 Jan. 1994).

Thomson, Barry. "Virtual Reality." Personal e-mail (25 Jan. 1995).

APPENDIX

Copyright Issues

Instructors increasingly have to work with copyright considerations as they prepare their course material. The "fair use clause" of the US Copyright Act gives instructors some flexibility when it comes to using copyrighted materials in the classroom:

> Not withstanding the provisions of sections 106 and 106A [17 USCS §§ 106, 106A] the fair use of a copyrighted work, including such use by reproduction in copies or phonorecords or by any other means specified by that section, for purposes such as criticism, comment, news reporting, teaching (including multiple copies for classroom use), scholarship, or research, is not an infringement of copyright. In determining whether the use made of a work in any particular case is a fair use the factors to be considered shall include--

> * (1) the purpose and character of the use, including whether such use is of a commercial nature or is for nonprofit educational purposes;
> * (2) the nature of the copyrighted work;
> * (3) the amount and substantiality of the portion used in relation to the copyrighted work as a whole; and
> * (4) the effect of the use upon the potential market for or value of the copyrighted work.

> The fact that a work is unpublished shall not itself bar a finding of fair use if such finding is made upon consideration of all the above factors.

Under these guidelines, it is possible to make use of copyrighted materials for the purpose of instruction. However, the inter-connectedness and spontaneous nature of the net complicates the notion of what constitutes the fair use of copyrighted materials. For example, duplicating an essay or an ad from a magazine for use in class might fall under the guidelines for fair use of copyrighted material because it is done for scholarly or critical purposes and not intended to make a profit. Posting the same material to a class newsgroup, however, might not be acceptable because it would be available to an audience outside the classroom and this availability might diminish the value of the original document. Perhaps even sending the article as an e-mail message would have the same effect, since e-mail messages are often forwarded to secondary parties. Posting materials on the World Wide Web compounds the problem of fair use because most Web browsers allow users to download any materials they find and to incorporate the source documents of Web pages into their own sites.

Because of the simplicity of distributing materials on the net, making clear distinctions about the boundaries of copyrighted materials becomes difficult. The rights of intellectual property owners should be balanced with those of individuals who wish to participate in the free-exchange of ideas. In their statement, "Fair Use in the Electronic Age: Serving the Public Interest" the American Library Association suggests that the balance between the owner's claims to intellectual property and the public's interest in the free exchange of ideas should be honored in electronic space.

> The primary objective of copyright is not to reward the labor of authors, but "[t]o promote the Progress of Science and useful Arts." To this end, copyright assures authors the right to their original expression, but encourages others to build freely upon the ideas and information conveyed by a work....This result is neither unfair nor unfortunate. It is the means by which copyright advances the progress of science and art. -- Justice Sandra Day O'Connor (Feist Publications, Inc. v. Rural Telephone Service Co., 499 US 340, 349 (1991) The genius of United States copyright law is that, in conformance with its constitutional foundation, it balances the intellectual property interests of authors, publishers and copyright owners with society's need for the free exchange of ideas.

The guidelines of the fair use clause can be applied to the Internet as well, but many of the issues relating to electronic use of material and particularly electronic scholarly use, are still unresolved. Some guidelines include using no more materials than necessary to make a given point or to develop an idea and considering whether using materials will devalue them in any way for the owner.

You will also find some material already online which probably shouldn't be, for example scanned pictures, unauthorized reproductions of texts, film clips and sound files. When evaluating sources, you consider the implications of using materials which are available online but which may not be in the public domain and strive to comply with fair use guidelines. Likewise, there are no mechanisms in place on the Internet for assuring that the material you post online won't at some point be downloaded and made use of in less than responsible ways.

GLOSSARY

Anchor 1.) the beginning point for a hypertextual link. Anchors usually use highlighted sections of text (hot text) or images to indicate links. 2.) in Web terminology, sometimes refers to the target destination for a link.

Application any type of commercial, shareware or freeware computer program (usually with a user interface).

Archie a protocol which allows keyword searches of the contents of FTP sites (primarily for names of freeware and shareware applications and graphic files).

ASCII Text also known as "text only" format, ASCII characters are the basic numbers, letters and symbols supported by most types of computer operating systems.

AU a sound file format commonly found on the World Wide Web.

Bookmark an electronic pointer to a Gopher, FTP or Web site that can be recalled for future reference. A list of bookmarks is known as a "hotlist."

Boolean 1.) logical search operators that allow a user to refine the scope of keyword searches. The simple Boolean operators are and, or, and not. 2.) flavoring used to make soup stock. Often small children will lick a Boolean cube for the salty flavor.

Bots (robots) objects in MOO environments which are programmed to interact with readers.

Channel also referred to as a "line." An IRC channel is roughly equivalent to a C.B. radio frequency. Users join a channel to participate in the discussion that takes place among people logged on to that frequency.

Chat 1.) a somewhat derogatory term used to describe newsgroups or listservs that are geared towards the discussion of nonacademic topics. 2.) a term often heard when talking about Internet Relay Chat (IRC). The IRC channels are often called "chat lines" and the conversations that take place on these channels are often referred to as "chat."

Clarinet newsfeeds from Rueters and the Associated Press in the form of Usenet newsgroups. Institutions must pay a fee in order to subscribe to groups provided by the Clarinet company.

Client Software software which communicates with a server to provide an easier interface for a user.

Common Gateway Interface (CGI) a program which resides on a server and handles complex information requests. CGIs act as mediators between a source of information on a server, and a client. They are most commonly used to process forms in HTML.

Directory a particular section of the basic organizational structure of a file system (known as a "folder" in some operating systems). Directories can contain any type of files, applications or other directories.

Domain an element of an Internet or e-mail address designating an Internet organization, sub-organizations and the type of organization (e.g., widgetinc.com, or utexas.edu).

DOS see *Operating System*.

Downloading retrieving a file or application from a remote host over the Internet.

E-mail (Electronic Mail) the basic form of Internet communication. E-mail is used to send all types of electronic correspondence to Internet-connected users around the world.

Emote to virtually represent an action during the real-time conversations on IRCs and MOOs. For example, a user named Socrates could type ":listens intently." and the text transmitted to other participants would read "Socrates listens intently."

Emoticons "pictures" made of text symbols that express different emotions in e-mail messages, newsgroup postings, and real time discussions. The basic Internet emoticon is the "smiley," a sideways happy face. :-)

FAQ (Frequently Asked Questions) a file which collects and responds to some of the most common questions about a particular aspect of the Internet or about a particular topic (e.g., the FAQ file for BMW motorcycles).

File any type of electronic document. Files can be in ASCII text, in a format for a particular program, or in a standardized format for sound, graphics or video (e.g., WAV, GIF, or MPEG).

Flame usually a pejorative term describing a post that attacks a message or an individual. A flame usually has a confrontational tone and offers little or no constructive criticism.

Form see *HTML Form*.

FTP (File Transfer Protocol) an early system of downloading and uploading files across the Internet. Although somewhat basic, FTP is still frequently used.

Freeware software distributed free of charge.

GIF Graphical Interchange Format a graphics file format that is frequently used for images on the World Wide Web.

Gopher a system of Internet protocols and directory structures that allows users to connect to remote hosts, to access directories of information and to download files. In addition, Gopher sites can be searched for directory names, file titles or text contained in individual files.

Gopher Client a program which provides an easy interface for searching and accessing documents and directories in Gopherspace.

Gopherhost see *Gopher Server*.

Gopher Server also referred to as a "Gopherhost." A centralized server that offers hierarchically organized information to a user via a Gopher client.

Hardware the mechanical parts of a computer system.

Hit an item returned from a keyword search.

Home Page conventional name given to a central site on the World Wide Web. This name can be used both for the central page of a university or business site and for the personal page of an individual.

Host 1.) an Internet-connected machine which serves files to various clients. 2.) Any Internet-connected machine.

Hot Text a hypertextual term which refers to a link anchored by a section of text. This is the most common way of linking documents on the Web. Hot text will generally appear in a different color or different style to indicate that clicking on it will take the user to another document.

Hotlist see *Bookmark*.

HTML (Hypertext Markup Language) the scripting language which is used to turn plain text and other elements (such as images) into the integrated pages we see on the Web.

HTML Elements HTML instructions, along with the text to which they apply; for example, the boldface text element, <B> this text will be bold </B>, and the table element, <TABLE> . . . </TABLE>. Some HTML elements are "empty," meaning they do not have an ending tag or perform a function on particular text; for example, the <HR> element draws a horizontal rule across the page.

HTML Form mechanism by which Web browsers allow users to send information back to a server. Forms can be used in a writing class to facilitate interaction between readers and authors of Web documents.

HTML Headings HTML commands which change the size of the text displayed in Web pages. Headings vary in size from <H1> through <H6> (largest to smallest).

HTML Tags HTML commands contained in angled brackets. Tags usually work in pairs, with a closing tag dictating where the selected text ends, but "empty" HTML elements, such as <HR>, do not have a closing tag.

HTTP (Hypertext Transport Protocol) an Internet protocol which allows for the transfer of files from a Web server to a Web client application.

Hypertexts interactive documents that allow users to follow links to other documents and to present images, sound, and video.

Imagemap an image which has been "mapped" by HTML commands so that clicking on different portions of it will link the user to different sites or files.

Index Page the initial page of a site (or of a series of documents) which provides the organizational structure that maps the site--often the "starting point" for a hypertext.

Inline Image an image which has been inserted into the design of a Web page.

Interface the features of an application which mediate a user 's interaction with the program. Generally speaking, the more intuitive the interface is to a user, the easier it will be to run the program.

IP Address (Internet Protocol Address) the address which is specific to a single computer and identifies it for the purpose of interacting with other computers on the Internet.

IRC (Internet Relay Chat) a system of Internet protocols and programs which allow users to participate on topic-centered, real-time discussion channels.

IRC Client a program which provides an easy interface for a user who is logged onto an IRC channel.

Java a programming language which grew out experiments in software to connect different types of servers. Supported by Netscape and other browsers, Java is the basis of many interactive functions on Web pages, such as moving animations and the managing of complex information. These functions are actually performed by applications, or "applets," which reside on servers rather than individual PCs.

JPG/JPEG (from Joint Photographic Experts Group) a graphics file format that is frequently used for images on the World Wide Web.

Link a hypertextual function that connects documents, sites, and other media. Note that "link" is commonly used both as a noun to indicate the actual connection between one node and another, and as a verb to indicate the process by which this connection is achieved.

Listproc a type of mailing list software. See also *Listserv*.

Listserv also known as a "mailing list" or "list." A program which allows mail to be sent to a group of addresses at once.

Local Area Network (LAN) a set of connections which allows a number of computers in a particular location to share files with each other. Most computer classrooms will be connected with a local area network.

Lurk to read a newsgroup or e-mail list for a period of time without posting messages. (This process is known as "lurking" because your presence is not known to the group unless you "speak up").

MacintoshÆ see *Operating System*. See also *Platform*.

Mail Reader also known as a "mail client." A program which provides an easy interface for reading, composing, posting and downloading e-mail messages.

Mail Server an Internet connected server which organizes, stores and distributes e-mail messages to various users.

Mailbox the specific identification or name given to an e-mail user. Used in conjunction with the domain name, it makes up the e-mail address.

Majordomo a type of mailing list software. See also *Listserv*.

Menu Command a command that is executed by using a mouse to click on an option within a menu bar, a feature of both Macintosh and Windows^Ÿ operating systems.

Modem short for "modulater-demodulater," a device used to connect computers via a telephone line or other communication link to a

network server. When you connect to the Internet at school your workstation may be directly wired to a server, but if you connect at home you will most likely need to use a modem.

Moderator person responsible for determining the relevancy of messages posted to a moderated newsgroup or e-mail discussion list. A moderator will forward "appropriate" messages to the group.

Multipurpose Internet Mail Extensions (MIME) an encoding format which allows for the transfer of mixed-media data by electronic mail.

MUDs (also MUSHs, Tiny MUSHs, MOOs, etc.) text-based virtual spaces ("Multi User Dungeons" or "Domains") which allow users to interact in real-time with other users or with the textual environment. The different acronyms refer to different programs which perform similar functions. MUD Client a program which provides an easy interface for a user who is logged onto a MUD.

MOV/MOOV a video format often used on the World Wide Web.

MPG/MPEG a video format often used on the World Wide Web.

News Host see *News Server*.

News Server also known as "News Host." An Internet connected server which organizes, stores and distributes newsgroup messages.

Newsfeed messages posted to a newsgroup which originate from a wire service or other traditional news source.

Newsgroups topic-centered sites devoted to discussion and to the exchange of articles, messages, or other media. See also *Usenet*.

Newsreader also known as a "news client." A program which provides an easy interface for reading, composing, posting and downloading newsgroup messages.

Nickname 1.) similar to an address book entry for one or more e-mail addresses. When a message is sent to the nickname the computer sends that message to each of the addresses in the nickname file. 2.) a character name used to log on to IRC channels.

Node a hypertextual site which organizes multiple links. Nodes can contain any combination of text, links, graphics, sound, and video.

Operating System the software which controls the basic operations of the computer. Examples include Macintosh, DOS, and Unix. These systems are generally incompatible with each other.

PC 1.) also referred to as "IBM compatibles," indicates computers which run DOSÆ operating systems (usually with the graphical user interface Windows). 2.) less often used to indicate any personal computer.

Platforms refers to computers with different types of operating systems, for example, Macintosh, PC, or Unix.

Post to send an electronic message to an e-mail discussion list or newsgroup. Also used as a noun to refer to the message itself.

Protocols the "language" that a client and server use to distinguish various types of Internet media. E-mail, for example, relies on Simple Mail Transfer Protocol (SMTP), while the Web uses Hypertext Transfer Protocol (HTTP).

Read-Only Memory (ROM) Information stored in chips or other media (e.g. CD-ROMS) that can only be read by a computer, not altered or written over.

Readme File gives information about a piece of software or an Internet forum.

Real-time refers to the almost instantaneous transfer of messages in IRCs and MOOs, allowing users to communicate in a way which resembles face-to-face conversation. Real-time can be seen in opposition to e-mail and newsgroup messages, which are asynchronous.

Reply Quotations instead of using quotation marks or a block quote, most mail readers and newsreaders place a special character, usually an angled bracket (>), in front of a quotation in order to distinguish it from a new message. Most mail readers and newsreaders offer a "reply" function which will quote the whole text of the original message using this special character.

Robot see *Bots*. Root Directory the uppermost directory in a directory hierarchy, designated by the slash symbol (/) in UNIX and HTTP.

Scroll to move up or down in a document using either the arrow keys or a mouse-driven scroll bar.

Search Engine a device that performs keyword searches on the Internet (e.g. Veronica, WAIS, WebCrawler).

Server 1.) simply put, software that provides information to client programs. Clients and servers "talk" to each other to allow the transfer of files and protocols across the Internet. 2.) commonly refers to the machine on which a server program is located.

Shareware like "freeware," software which is made available through the Internet. The authors of shareware ask for a small fee from users.

Signature File pre-formatted text attached to the bottom of most e-mail and newsgroup messages which generally contains the author's name, e-mail address, and institutional affiliation (if any). Signature files often contain carefully constructed ASCII text pictures and favorite quotations.

Site License an agreement which allows an organization to own and operate multiple copies of the same program.

Site a collection of documents on the Internet providing information to users who access the location. Gopher sites and Web sites are the "places" designed by particular people or institutions to disseminate information (used to describe both a "home page" and a "host").

Slide Show a series of textual screens that scroll by to deliver information in a MOO.

Software computer programs written to perform various tasks, as opposed to "hardware" which refers to the mechanical parts of a computer system. See also *Application*.

Source Document the underlying HTML document that produces a Web page when viewed with a Web browser. Most Web browsers allow a user to "view" the source document of any page found on the Web.

Subject Directory hypertext index of Internet resources categorized by subject; featured on Gopher and Web research tools.

Surfing the process of navigating from site to site on the Internet (usually the Web) in a nonlinear and non-hierarchical manner.

Targeting connecting directly to a Gopherhost or Web site by entering a known address.

Telnet a terminal emulation protocol. With a Telnet client application, you can establish a connection to a remote computer. Telnet refers both to the process of making "terminal emulation" connections on the Internet, and to the client applications which perform this function, such as NCSA Telnet.

Text Only see *ASCII Text*.

Thread a posting and a series of replies on the same topic, usually with the same subject heading.

Tunneling accessing a site (usually a Gopher site) by digging down through various directories or sub-directories.

Unix see *Operating System*. See also *Platform*.

Uploading placing a file or application on a remote host over the Internet. Often used to put text, sound, graphics, video, and HTML files on a Web server for publication.

URL (Uniform Resource Locator) the address assigned to each file on the World Wide Web.

Usenet one subset of the Internet which facilitates the exchange of messages and discussion. Most colleges and universities are involved with Usenet newsgroups rather than private or commercial bulletin boards. The broad classification of Usenet contains thousands of topic-centered newsgroups organized hierarchically by name.

Veronica a search engine which can locate items on most of the Internet's Gopher servers using keywords and Boolean operators.

WAIS (Wide Area Information Search) a search engine configured to locate and retrieve information from a designated set of documents. Unlike Veronica or the Web search engines, WAIS performs local rather than general Internet searches. WAV a sound file format.

Web Browser client software used for navigating and interacting with the World Wide Web. The Web browser translates the HTML source documents that reside on the Web into a fluid, multimedia interface.

Web Server a server equipped with software to facilitate the Hypertext Transfer Protocol (HTTP) that enables documents to be linked and shared on the Web. Users can access the documents stored on Web servers with a Web browser.

Windows see *Operating System*.

Workstation an individual computer usually connected to a network but primarily occupied by a single user. Used throughout this book to designate a personal computer where a user can operate local client software.

World Wide Web abbreviated "WWW" or "the Web." Distributed hypermedia system built upon older protocols (FTP, Gopher, etc.) and additional newer protocols (HTTP).

WWW client software (see *Web Browser*) provides the ability to view many types of files (HTML, GIF, text, etc.).

INDEX